# What One Man Saw

## Being the Personal Impressions
## of a War Correspondent
## in Cuba

by

## Harrie Irving Hancock

The Clapton Press

# What One Man Saw

*BEING THE PERSONAL IMPRESSIONS
OF A WAR CORRESPONDENT
IN CUBA*

BY

H. IRVING HANCOCK

NEW YORK
STREET & SMITH, Publishers
238 WILLIAM STREET

# Contents

# Introduction

Harrie Irving Hancock was born in Massachusetts in 1868 or thereabouts. He was a chemist, a journalist and a prolific author of children's books, writing more than fifty adventure stories targetted at adolescent boys, including a four part series depicting a German invasion of the United States published in 1916, a year before his country entered the First World War. He also wrote a number of non-fiction works, including targeted reports on the American war against Spain in Cuba and the Philippines. He died in 1922 from disease of the liver.

*What One Man Saw* was published in 1898, shortly after Cuba and the Philippines won their independence from Spain, with considerable assistance from the United States which, during the course of the 19th century, had replaced Spain as Cuba's principal trading partner. The United States had long had designs on Cuba, even offering to purchase the island from Spain in 1854, for a consideration of up to USD120 million.

Cuba's third war of independence had begun in February 1895. The US declared war on Spain in April 1898 and by August the war had been won, signalling the start of a four year occupation of the island by its northern neighbour, following which the US retained a legal right to intervene militarily in the islands to protect its interests, a right that it exercised by sending in the Marines from 1906-1909, in 1912, from 1917-1922 and again, unsuccessfully, in 1961.

Hancock's text is reproduced here unexpurgated; for avoidance of doubt that does not mean that any of his views or prejudices (prevalent at the time) are shared by the undersigned or by the publishers.

George Nichols

# CAMPAIGNING IN CUBA

---

# Chapter I

# The First Dark Night at Sea

"If anyone tells a ghost story," said the Major, "he will be fined six months' pay."

"And the enemy to our peace of mind who repeats the tale of the Flying Dutchman," amended the Colonel, "will be thrown overboard."

The major was a retired army officer who, being now unable to serve the flag, laid aside the sword for the pen. "Colonel" was a title which the possessor had won in a civic way. He was a newspaper proprietor from Iowa who had resolved up being his own war correspondent. We were all war correspondents, and there were thirty-four of us on board the *Olivette*. One, a German, had seen the Japo-Chinese war. An Englishman present had accompanied one of England's punitive expeditions into Africa. The other thirty-two of us were strictly raw material. That was why we felt so strange and eerie on an utterly dark ship.

Have you ever spent an entire evening on a ship where not one ray of light shows? Probably not. It isn't a common experience; but the *Olivette* was proceeding strictly under orders. It was a dark night, and inclined to be foggy. The *Olivette* was steaming fast over the slightly rolling waters of the Gulf. She had orders to overtake Shafter's fleet at Rebecca Light, down by Dry Tortugas way. Yet to go in this fashion, without a light showing anywhere on board—it was weird, and somehow impressed the victim as not being strictly honest.

"It makes me feel like a pirate to go sneaking through the night in this fashion," remarked the Major.

On the afterdeck, where we sat, no man in the group could see another's face. Up on the hurricane deck, where some of us afterward went, and where the fog seemed more enveloping, the effect of the vague, dim, moving figures was peculiarly spectral. Groping our way through the salons, we almost invariably ran into each other until we learned to keep our voices sounding, after the fashion of ships moving through a fog. Only when we supposed ourselves to be in front of the doors of our respective staterooms were we allowed to strike a match for the purpose of scanning the numbered tablet over the door. Then the match must be blown out at once. This was all in the agreement that we had signed that afternoon at the instance of the army surgeon who acted as the ship's military commander. But we were inclined to be happy and contented. We were off at last, bound for Cuba with Shafter's expedition, and this was an achievement for which most of us had waited many weeks at Tampa.

The expedition was ready to sail on the eighth of June. All that day transport steamers pulled out of the canal at Port

Tampa and, with riggings full of cheerful soldiers and bands playing stirring melodies, steamed slowly down the bay to form. Everybody felt sure that the expedition was under way, but toward night the ships began warping into the canal. The expedition was called back, yet why? Gradually it leaked out that two strange Spanish warships had been seen in Nicholas Channel. Orders from Washington had delayed the start. The delay lasted six days.

Finally, on the fourteenth, the huge transport fleet got away, the ships leaving singly, and it was not until dark that the last of them steamed out of the port and down the tortuous windings of the bay. Even then the *Olivette* did not start. She had been over to St Petersburg all day, taking aboard water for, in addition to being the hospital ship and press yacht, the Olivette also performed the functions of water boat. At night, Tuesday, we found ourselves tied up to a pier at Port Tampa, taking aboard coal for the cruise. It was early Wednesday morning when we started. The *Olivette*, however, was swift, and eleven o'clock that lightless Wednesday night found us steaming into the thick of Shafter's waiting fleet as dark and spectral as ourselves.

We were part of the expedition at last. It was worth a good deal to know this, and knowing it we were content to go to bed. Most of the correspondents were berthed in staterooms on the main deck. Down into that Stygian darkness we groped our way by staircases. Bump! I ran into another fellow a good deal larger than myself, fell back in good order against a post, and next sat down on the floor with jarring concussion.

"Why didn't you blow your foghorn oftener?" was all the satisfaction I got. A twinkling of little match lights all along the main deck showed a whole galaxy of correspondents in doubt about the exact locations of their staterooms. Five minutes later we were in our berths and trying to sleep. But it was hot on that main deck. Besides, up forward on the same deck were the stalls of horse, and the mingling of stable smells that came back had not the sedative effect of Araby's balmy odors. Yet it is safe to say we were all asleep when the fleet got under way at some time about daylight. A quick toilet, a rush for deck, and what a sight was there!

Ahead, astern, and in a long line to starboard were transports. The fleet was moving in two lines, at general intervals of about a thousand feet. Away off to the starboard steamed the *Osceola*, a two-funneled tug which the Government had hurriedly converted into a gunboat. Her armament was a few light guns, yet already on the Cuban blockage her commander had gained a reputation for trying to make his craft do the work of a battleship. Right in her wake followed that business-like craft, the torpedo boat *Ericsson*. On the starboard of the fleet rode the *Indiana*, looking like a mighty castle floating on the water. In her wake was another torpedo boat. Further down on the starboard line of the fleet were the *Detroit* and two gunboats, while still further astern were other craft that we could hardly make out—a total of thirty-six transports and fifteen naval. A lazy Armada! Rolling along over the low swell, we seldom made more than seven knots an hour. Yet it looked like business, with the naval craft scooting here and there, the transports with their decks crowded with soldiers, with bands playing and with all the ships wig-wagging signals to each other from their bridges until, to the uninitiated, it seemed as if the whole Armada were going mad from the confusion of orders.

Even the most inspiring scenes pall at last. We found ourselves breaking up into little groups. Captain Silva, a picturesque young Cuban officer, holding a folded newspaper before him, showed one knot of writers how the signal corps wig-wags daylight messages by the aid of the signal flag. Other groups read or smoked in silence, while a few correspondents brought out notebooks and wrote industriously. There were even a few who found it interesting to gaze for an hour or two more at the five-mile-long fleet carrying the first invasionary expedition in Uncle Sam's history. But it was a bright genius who suddenly conceived the idea of organizing the "Board of Strategy." Lest there may be readers who do not understand clearly the proceedings of such a board, I will merely hint that the deliberations are conducted with the aid of celluloid chips. One of the standard maxims in this branch of strategy is that "three of a kind beat two pair." The "Board of Strategy" was almost continuously in session during the daylight hours of the rest of the voyage, for the kind of men who go voluntarily on fight expeditions to other countries are not the kind of men whom a little rough weather affects.

Toward noon we passed the Cape Lobos lighthouse. The cape is the southernmost end of one of the British West

Indian islands. There were only three or four other houses in sight, but certain it must be that the lightkeeper and all of the other villagers were up in the great white tower. I would give a great deal to know what those Britons thought while they were gazing out on the great American Armada. We soon had other things to think of, for we were nearing Cayo Romano. Here there were known to be four Spanish *canoneros*, or gunboats, driven up shallow streams by American war vessels. Insignificant craft no doubt they were, though quite capable of destroying any transports upon which they could come unawares.

# Chapter II
# War at Long Range

What does this mean? There is sudden, puzzling activity in the fleet. Until now the *Osceola* has been on our port bow, with a torpedo boat following her. Now the *Indiana*—though occupying the same position, for castles, even floating ones, are hard to move—has both torpedo boats close to her, and the *Osceola* is just dead ahead of us, suggesting a marine bulldog with the comforting suggestion that no mishap shall be allowed to befall the purveyors of news aboard the *Olivette*. Another gunboat is hurrying to the front, while the Hornet takes up a position on our starboard quarter, toward the Cuban coast, and hangs tenaciously to us. What is up? It is evident that something is happening out of the usual. Uncle Sam's tars are not easily rattled; they do not crowd on extra steam for nothing. And so the excitement grows, feeding on the indications of lurking trouble. Some of the transports are putting out to sea, their Captains giving Cuba a wider berth, though all along that anarchy-pervaded island has been literally out of sight.

But the *Olivette* betrays no cowardice. It would be base ingratitude to be afraid when we are so surrounded by fine fighting craft manned by our gallant Jackies. There is furious wig-wagging going on on the hurricane deck of the Osceola and Captain Stevens, an army signal officer, is on the bridge of the Olivette reading the signal. We look at him wistfully, but ask no questions. We have tried him before, and have found him a safe custodian of the signalled secrets. The excitement grows, until Spain's four *canoneros* assume the imaginative aspect of battleships. But what have we to fear, after all? The newsgatherers on the Olivette are now enjoying the vigilant protection of nearly half the vessels in the naval convoy. Under such championship we become indifferent. Four Spanish *canoneros*? Bah! An hour later the excitement is over, and the fleet is sailing once more in its usual formation. A suspicious cloud of smoke, away on the horizon over by Cayo Romano, had been perceived by the lookout on the foremost naval vessel. The manoeuvers we have seen were merely precautions. Who was afraid? The "Board of Strategy" calls for more chips. An hour later we learn that the sudden massing of warships nearby was not at all for the protection of the press, but for the safety of General Shafter's flagship, the *Segurança*, which, at the time , as running abeam of us.

There are no more alarms by day. Dark comes, and the word should be spelled in capitals, for dark means DARK on the Olivette, as on most of the other ships of the fleet. The starts are brighter in the tropics than in the more northern latitudes. On the Olivette even starlight is at a premium. We gather on the hurricane deck and light our pipes. All hands are smoking comfortably when the youngster from Cincinnati, who always sees everything, suddenly exclaims:

"There goes a red rocket!"

He is right. Even as we turn to look a second ascends. Both come from the naval vessel that is acting as guide to the fleet. Two red rockets constitute the danger signal. There is a clanging of bells in engine rooms, and the big transports gradually stop, content to drift lazily. Only the naval vessels keep on ahead, undisturbed. The gunboat that sent up the rocket displays a sudden burst of colored lights near her masthead. Swiftly the lights change as to position and colors, then change again and again. Electric signal lights blaze out, as quickly subsiding, and other naval vessels pass the intelligence—whatever it is—along the five-mile line of the fleet. Night signalling at sea is a wonderfully pretty sight, but mystifying, utterly bewildering to the greenhorn. But pshaw! It is another bugaboo—"more spookships", as we say when the fleet gets under way again. Yet this sort of thing is wearing on the nerves. We are not afraid to die, but prefer to do it on land.

Saturday morning there is a long halt. We have stopped for a rendezvous every morning, but this is a genuine "get-together-boys" and takes a long while, for during the night many of the ships have lagged, and now the fleet looks long-drawn-out and disorganized. We have got to get in closer formation and keep it. The soldier who wags the signal flag on the *Segurança's* bridge is sending back scolding messages to the captains of the transports that caused this unusual delay. In the interim many of the transports are lowering small boats and sending their sick soldiers to the *Olivette*. Typhoid fever and measles have caught about even numbers of the soldiers. After two or three hours the great Armada steams slowly on again. Army men and the foreign military attachés discuss the possibilities of our falling in with Admiral Camara's Cadiz squadron, which had sailed mysteriously from Spain several days before we left Port Tampa. There has been time for it to get to these waters by now, though the big *Indiana*, with a crew so long trained by Captain Bob Evans, seems capable of coping with a whole Spanish fleet. But no adventures come our way.

Sunday brings a little break in the monotony. It is found that the *Gussie* is out of water. The *Gussie* is an old red side-wheeler, of a type long obsolete, but Uncle Sam took her for a transport. The *Gussie* is loaded with mules and Arizona cowboys. It is the mules that want the water. The *Olivette* has plenty to spare, but out here at sea it is too rough for the vessels to get near enough. So we are ordered to proceed to Inagua, a little British island. As we leave the fleet we see that the great procession wheels suddenly to the southward. This means the Windward Passage, and a great hurrah goes up, for if the ships are going through the Windward they are bound for no other place than Santiago de Cuba. We had left Tampa in the dark as to our exact destination, but now we are happy. "If we were going to Puerto Rico," explains Dr Diaz, of the Baptist Church of Havana, who is aboard, "there would be no fight, for this expedition could catch all the Spaniards in Puerto Rico by throwing the hat," a performance which he illustrates with a graphic Latin gesture. "But at Santiago— well, there will not be much of a fight, but the Spaniards will have no excuse that they were whipped by a foe of greatly superior numbers."

Now that the destination is settled we go forward and watch for the first glimpse of British territory. It is not long before land is sighted, nor much longer before we are at rest in the harbor of the principal village of the island of Inagua, with three gunboats waiting to convoy us out to sea again. It is a pretty place, of the tropical order, with cool-looking white houses and plenty of spreading palms. We espy an English flag on shore, and salute it with our hats. Then we make out Old Glory, and salute it twice. Meanwhile the *Gussie* and the *Olivette* have been connected by a large hose passed over the sterns of both ships, and water is pumped aboard the *Gussie* at the rate of a good many gallons to the minute. A boat manned by two darkies of the Jamaica type, and steered by a colored boy in a naval cadet's uniform, puts out from shore and comes alongside. There is a passenger who comes aboard and proves to be the local postmaster, customs-house officer and general British *Pooh-Bah*. He is a pleasant young fellow and, learning that he is not needed in an official capacity, he remains for nearly an hour in a social way, answering all our questions about the island, and finally offering to take as many of us ashore as his boat will hold. But it will only be three. As a consolation to the rest, he promises to send out several bumboatmen—a promise which he keeps, and soon we are buying cigars, bananas and pineapples from the navigators of a dozen small boats that ply alongside.

In a little while the three fortunate correspondents come

back from shore. They have plenty to tell us about the indolent *dolce far niente* life of the place, offsetting this with the fact that there are some two hundred lepers on the island who are not isolated from the remainder of the population. Some of us cannot help looking at the cigars we are smoking, and wondering whether they are genuine "leper hand-made." There is water enough on the *Gussie* now for the mules, and other comforts for the Arizona contingent. There with friendly toots of the whistle for the courteous residents who stand on the shore waving hats and handkerchiefs to us, we leave Inagua behind.

It is dark when we get into the Windward Passage, and beyond the fact that the water is rough, this famous channel makes no impression on us until we near Cape Maysi. Here, at a ticklish point for navigators, the Spanish light is burning brightly. A false beacon perhaps, decided several of the quick-witted correspondents, and one of our number hurries off to suggest the notion to Captain Stevenson, who had already thought of the same thing, and is relying upon his compass instead of the light. But weeks later we learned that the Spanish lighthouse keeper actually had not learned of the war, and therefore kept his wick trimmed brightly and well-turned up to light the fleet that was carrying Spain's doom with it!

"Santiago in the morning," is the thought in every man's mind as he turns in. That is why we are all astir earlier than usual in the morning; but the Olivette is still under way, almost at the tail of the fleet, with which she has just caught up. Those who have port staterooms can see the grand mountains just back of the Cuban coast while we dress. We are not more than five or six miles from shore. We have already passed Guantanamo, where our marines are so easily standing off a superior force of Spain's soldiers. We are not near Santiago, however, and so breakfast is welcome as a stop-gap. These breakfasts have been getting worse and worse, so we do not waste much time in the salon, but hurry out on deck once more.

By and by we discover some naval vessels that do not belong to our convoy. They are the first of the great semi-circle of Sampsons's and Schley's war vessels that surround the approach to Santiago. There is a cheering and brave show of cameras. We expect to soon be on shore, and therefore when the purser appears he is volleyed with questions as to our weapons. We thirty-four are the owners of weapons enough to arm a pirate crew, but owing to the fact that the Olivette flies the hospital flag our combined arsenal has been locked up in one of the purser's closets all the way down. His replies now show that we are not likely to get our death-dealing apparatus right away. We come to anchor some eight or ten miles away from Morro, and there we drift about through the day. Toward dark, by climbing up in the rigging and using field glasses, we are able to see some of our warships sail into the mouth of the harbor, there to give the enemy the usual fifteen minutes' worriment before night. We see puffs of smoke, but that is all. It is war at long range.

# Chapter III
# The Landing at Daiquiri

There were tragedy in the air that Monday night when we sat down at dinner off Santiago. It came upon us all unawares. The meal set before us was undeniably bad. The soup appeared to have been made from left-over scraps of canned meat. We ate that, and waited for the next course. Over at the centre table, where the captain of the vessel and the surgeon-major in command sat, at least two mouths were watering. Before leaving Port Tampa the captain had secured the only turkey to be found. This had been kept religiously on ice. It was a compact between the surgeon-major and the captain that when they reached Cuba this fowl should be served up in state. They two would eat the turkey. Perhaps some of the foreign military attachés would be asked to have a taste, but the correspondents were not in the calculation at all. We were blissfully ignorant of the plot until the captain's boy, going up to the pantry, called briskly out: "De cap'n says have his turkey sent up."

"Send up the captain's turkey," shouted the steward's more cautious voice at the pipe. There was a moment's pause, and then up through the pipe from the lower regions came a wailing voice:

" 'Fore Gawd, somebody done stole dat cap'n's turkey!"

The agonized cry traveled all the way up to where the captain and the surgeon-major sat. Their faces were far more than I can describe. Here was one of the real hardships of war. An investigation was at once ordered. The steward was sent below to conduct it. He found no trace of the turkey, and, when he came back, could only explain that the cook had turned his back for a minute upon the open door of the oven in which the fowl had just finished browning. When the cook carried the platter to the oven he found the turkey gone. The trail of grease stopped at the galley door. There was no clue. The captain and the major looked at each other. Then one of them said in a strained voice, "Will you please pass the canned corn beef?"

Whether or not it was to discourage thievery the electric lights were turned on full that night. It was a blessing that those who have not been deprived of it for five nights in succession cannot appreciate. The "Board of Strategy" held an early all-night session. But we were all up early in the morning, for surely a landing was to be made. We were mistaken. The great fleet cruised about, but not all the arrangements had been made between Shafter and Sampson, and so Tuesday went by without a soldier being put ashore. The surgeon-major improved the time by mustering all the privates and non-commissioned officers of his hospital corps on deck and reading to them a stern lecture on thieving, supplementing it by the dreadful information that in time of war the extreme penalty for stealing was death. He never found out what became of the turkey. The correspondents did.

That fowl was confiscated and picked clean by some of the grimy stokers, who believed that the hardest-worked men needed the best food. At this late day there can be no harm in giving this much of a clue to the mystery, and I may add that the correspondents leaned largely to sympathy with the stokers.

Wednesday morning we awoke to find ourselves steaming eastward. By the time the majority got on deck the *Olivette* was steaming close to a village wrapped in flames. It was our landing place, Daiquiri, and the enemy had set as much as possible of it on fire. There were perhaps a dozen of the transports inshore. The remainder kept well out. At last we lay to. The triangle sounded for breakfast, but we ate quickly and little, like children who are going to the circus. Then we hurried out on deck again, crowding up in the bow to watch the shore. On land there was not a human being in sight. The ruins of the railroad roundhouse and some other buildings smouldered, but no token of human presence was given us. Were the Spaniards hiding, lying in wait for us? Were we to step peacefully on the beach, or would the grounding of the first boats develop a sudden whirlwind of bullets?

Boom! The first gun sounded. Down the coast at Siboney one of the naval vessels had opened fire on the town. There was a Spanish force there, skulking in the trenches, and back into the woods. It was the first shot we had heard in anger, and it sent eager blood in our bodies dancing. Through field glasses we could make out retreating bodies of the enemy. BANG! Right over to starboard of us one of the *New Orleans'* big guns talked thunderously. A great cloud of smoke hovered over her port side. Away up on the hill to the eastward of Daiquiri a sullen explosion answered a cloud of smoke belching out through the trees. Before we had caught our breath the cruiser *Detroit* and the gunboats *Wasp* and *Castine* were firing broadsides. From the hill came explosions and puffs of smoke innumerable. We were under fire at last. Spanish masked batteries were replying. That was what we thought, and we turned to the fleet to learn where, if anywhere, the Spanish gunners were scoring. That showed the folly of taking things for granted. Over the din of the furious bombardment the Major's voice could be heard explaining, in answer to the question of one of the correspondents:

"No, certainly we are not under fire. Those explosions and clouds of smoke on the hill show where our shells are landing."

"Why is our fleet firing?" I asked.

"For any one of several reasons. It may be to unmask a suspected Spanish position, or it may be that our naval officers have caught sight of a reconnoitering column of the enemy. Again, it may be that they have received news of a large intrenched force of the enemy over in the village."

We watched the brisk bombardment with renewed interest. I think most of us were secretly annoyed to find that we were not under fire. A bombardment is a splendid spectacular effect, but the Anglo-Saxon nature always does revolt at the idea of a one-sided fight. Probably that is why we hoped and therefore believed that a large Spanish force was concealed near the points at which our naval vessels were firing their shells. Upon the hill I have just mentioned was a blockhouse. Again and again athe navy's guns aimed at that structure, though not once did they hit it. So close inshore were the gunboats that the elevation was too great for them. But there was a blockhouse lower down, in the village, that our grim Jackies literally demolished. Then there was a prodigious amount of firing at the low bluffs along the shore. There were splendidly constructed rifle trenches along these bluffs, although from the decks of the transports we could see nothing of them, albeit they strongly commanded the beach where the landing was intended. In the midst of the furious firing we descried Admiral Sampson's flagship, the *New York*, swiftly approaching.

"When she gets her big batteries at work," was the word passed from mouth to mouth, "the Spaniards might as well go wind-jamming."

But the *New York*, without firing a shot, came on with the dignified reticence of a huge mastiff, stalking in among the small dogs of war with an air which seemed to ask:

"What is all this tremendous barking about?"

Just as suddenly as it had begun the bombardment stopped. It had lasted exactly fifteen minutes, and hundreds of shells had been fired. Should a Cuban wish to plant in Daiquiri, in the near future, he will hardly have to plough the land.

Out on the end of the iron pier belonging to the Spanish-American Iron Company appeared a solitary Cuban frantically waving a white cloth as a signal that the coast was clear of the enemy. Some thirty rowboats, towed by half a dozen naval tenders, now proceeded to the shore. Each boat was as full as it could be of soldiers in heavy marching order. A lusty cheer jarred the air as three boats leaped through the surf almost simultaneously, and a dozen soldiers were loudly arguing the question of who was first to step upon Cuban soil. Before it could possibly be settled, a half a dozen more boats had grounded, and the army was disembarking in earnest. As if by magic, Cubans now appeared on the beach. They were greeted with cheers and shouts of *"Viva Cuba libre,"* which they returned with loud yells of *"Vivan los americanos!"* The new allies seemed to be going wild with enthusiasm at that first meeting. Later on we discovered how much the Cuban part of it amounted to. Before the landing was over several of our soldiers upset and floundered in the water.

Cuban soldiers sat on the beach and looked on, while American Jack Tars went manfully to the rescue. Two of our men, sinking under the weight of their loaded cartridge belts and other pieces of equipment, were drowned—the first men lost on duty. Had our Cuban allies, who witnessed the scene practically unmoved, been quick to the resuce, these men might have been saved to fight before Santiago.

Along the southern Cuban coast the surf runs high. The beach is steep and the surf comes thundering in. There is force behind that thunder, and he is a capable navigator who can successfully beach a boat for several consecutive trips, as the littering of the beach with a half-dozen stove-in lifeboats quickly showed. There are no better handlers of boats in the world than our own Jack Tars, yet on the second day of landing an overturned, smashed-up launch added to the litter on the beach and testified to the capabilities of the Cuban surf.

It was early on the morning of the second day that the

correspondents were able to make arrangements for landing. It required several trips to get us ashore, for each man went sitting on top of his own particular baggage, while tents and general mess effects came later. As for the baggage, we left that piled up on the little wooden pier, under charge of our colored mess servants until the latter could arrange for its handling by Cuban packers. We were on Cuban soil. We raced onward to inspect Daiquiri. There wasn't much of it. Most of the village was under the shelter of a dozen primitive wooden buildings on an elevated bit of ground that overlooked the little narrow-gauge railway running down from the mountain to the pier.

But we made one discovery that was just what we were looking for—a Cuban regiment going through roll call. There were probably two hundred of them dressed, in general, in a kind of ecru-colored linen, the raggedest uniforms conceivable. Of the straw hats they wore, though it may sound like a bull, there is only one phrase that will do them justice, and that phrase is uniform non-descriptness. The shoes of the few who wore such articles were shapeless articles made, seemingly, from sailcloth. Their arms were the particular glory of the Cubans. These they had in great variety, as to style. There were Springfields, Winchesters, Marlins, Mausers and other makes—nearly all of them excellent guns. Ammunition, too, they had in quantities, contained in a succession of small cartridge boxes running around the belt. Not a Cuban in the "regiment" was without his machete. In addition, now, each wore over his back a gunny sack pouch well filled with Uncle

Sam's rations. They were of all ages, these Cubans, from fifteen to sixty, but every one had a lean and hungry look. None of them had the strong, sturdy look of our own people, yet these half-fed rebels could perform wonders in the way of long marches over the fearful mountain trails.

I was eager to have the opinion of my friend, the major-correspondent, of these insurgents from a military stand-point.

"Well," replied the Mayor, with a quizzical smile. "I guess they'll fight. I don't quite see how such ragged fellows can, with modesty, turn their backs on the enemy."

# Chapter IV
# The Invaders in Camp

*"Presente,"* answered each man as his name was called from the roll held by his company officer. Then, in a twinkling the word was given for the start. They moved off at a shuffling gait, like men who are weary-footed, passing down the hill into the low, flat valley beyond, and here they were quickly lost to sight among the trees.

"Where are they going?" we asked.

"Oh, only along the road a piece, to camp," was the answer.

Our informant was not well informed, for the Cubans marched straight over the mountain trails, some eight miles, until they ran into a Spanish force near Siboney. There was a fight in a second, and the Cubans fell back; sending couriers hot-foot for Yankee help. A brigade, already well out on the road, comprising the Eighth and Twenty-Second U.S. Infantry and the Second Massachusetts Volunteers, was hurried to their aid. We correspondents missed that fight, but it wasn't much of a fight, anyway, for the American brigade routed the Spaniards and took Siboney without the loss of a man, though the Cubans, owing to their precipitateness, had sixteen slightly wounded. Now, on the best information we could get, there would be no more fighting for days. Some of our regiments would be pushed as far as Siboney, and in the meantime the remainder of the troops, the artillery, wagons and mules, the commissary and other supplies were to be unloaded. Therefore, most of the correspondents selected a site on a level plateau overlooking the sea, and a mile and a quarter out of town. We shared the site with an artillery outpost under command of Lieutenant Altman. Here our tents were pitched, and camp life began in earnest. The artillery outpost was one in name only—there were no guns, only the men and some of the horses. The horses were coming ashore as fast as they could be unloaded from the transports. From our camp we could only see the work of unloading. There was only one way to get the horses ashore—to swim them. From an open port of a transport a wide, cleated gangplank would be rigged, leading down to the water. Down this the horse, blindfolded, and secured to the end of a long halter held from the stern of a rowboat, would be led. When he struck the water unexpectedly the horse was sure to swim. Perhaps half the distance to the shore he was towed by the halter, then blind and halter cast off and the animal left to find his own way to shore. Despite the heavy surf, most of the horses performed their part well, but a few were unavoidably drowned, and the carcasses piled up on the beach where we could see them and, later on, smell them.

Lieutenant Altman's men had not fared well at the commissary. On learning this we sent over to them a few cans of meat and other articles of food. Lieutenant Altman came over, introduced himself, and thanked us on behalf of his men. We found him a bright, energetic, splendid young fellow, though not in those respects different from almost all the other young army officers. Supper was an impromptu and not altogether satisfactory affair, but we were at the front, and therefore disposed to be happy.

Early in the evening we discovered what the rainy season in Cuba means. One lieutenant, four correspondents and a mule driver sat in a 7x7 tent in which most of the space was already monopolized by two cots and considerable baggage. By the dim light of a lantern belonging to the artillery we smoked, told stories and endeavored to forecast the campaign. When the rain let up, those who didn't berth in the tent departed.

Reveille brought us out of bed at daylight. Toilet and breakfast were both hurried through with, for now we were going to the front. Most of us started off over the mountain trail for Siboney that morning, and most of us, incidentally, came back. We were too heavily dressed, carried too heavy rolls, too great weight of rations, and were otherwise unfitted for the work of following a cowpath trail up one mountain and down it, then up another and down. It was scorching hot, our canteens were soon emptied, and the water we found in the mountain streams was too warm for immediate drinking purposes. My comrade and I decided to come back with our heavy belongings and make a fresh, lighter start.

A good many others came back before venturing as far out as we did. It was disappointing, but a valuable experience, for we learned in time that one must gradually accustom himself to mountain climbing in the tropics, that he must travel with the lightest possible pack, and most of all, that he must learn to do his traveling in the coolest hours of the day. All along the road we saw evidences that our troops did not intend to be hampered by too many things to carry. The road was strewn with blouses, blankets—in fact, every part of a soldier's outfit that could be dispensed with. Thousands and thousands of dollars were represented by these castaway things. Later on the Cubans got them.

While we were out on that trail the Rough Riders were in the thick of it at Las Guasimas. Not one of the corrrespondents who started out Friday morning was near enough to even hear the shots of that battle, or skirmish, as it has since been termed. But a courier who came in that night brought tidings which led us to believe that we were soon to witness a fight without the trouble of moving. Four hundred Spaniards, finding our advanced forces at Santiago, had taken to an unused trail, and were working toward Daiquiri through the jungle. If they could attack our outpost at night, and kill the artillery horses, besides perhaps destroying a part of our supplies at the Daiquiri base, it would be a brilliant achievement for them. Right ahead of us was a steep, cone-like hill, covered with the densest chaparral, from which such an attack could be easily made. Double sentries were posted, and we went to bed with an expectation of excitement before morning. I was just falling asleep near midnight when a shot sounded. It appeared to be less than a quarter of a mile away. Two more shots followed almost instantly. Thoroughly aroused, I sat up. On the cot opposite, a Canadian correspondent snored blissfully. On the ground between two cots lay another comrade. He was awake, as a restless move showed.

"What do you think of it?" I asked.

"There goes the alarm," he replied, as a bugle rang out. "And there goes the 'assembly' too. It begins to look like business." Indeed it did, for the next notes were those of "left front into line." Troops were forming to hunt the enemy! It struck us as strange that no one was stirring in the artillery camp. Ten minutes of restless, eager waiting followed. No shots were fired. Then came the "retreat," sounding nervous and irritable even on the bugle. No doubt that trumpeter was disgusted.

"No fight," grunted Brandenberg and went to sleep. There were other shots that night, but no attack. It is wearing on a fellow's nerves, at first, to hear shots every few minutes through the night, but he soon becomes used to it, and will sleep soundly under all but heavy firing.

With morning came an urgent necessity to move our camp. Those dead horses, piling up on the beach, protested against our staying—protested by filling the hot air with a stench that precluded any idea of eating breakfast on that spot.

Down came the tents, and off went the baggage. Our new camp was pitched over at Daiquiri, on the bluff overlooking the sea.

# Chapter V
# The Marvel of Spanish Trenches

Ten feet from the door of my tent ran an innocent-looking trench. Innocent? It was one of the death traps set for us by the Spaniards. Think of one of the narrow trenches sometimes dug in our streets when gas pipes are to be laid down. The Spanish trench is generally about three and a half feet deep. There is no dirt piled up in front of it. All that is carefully carted away and spread. When timbers are obtainable these are set in the top of the trench, flush with the surface of the ground. As a rule, the trench is not visible fifty yards away. Down in these trenches the little brown men drop, hide out of sight and wait—wait until the crop of Yankees is near enough for the harvest of death. Quick as a flash, when the word is given up bob the little brown heads, only two or three inches of each showing. Rifles begin to blaze all along the line. A short series of these trenches will hide five hundred men, their handy little Mausers will shoot thirty to the minute—and there you are! Fifteen thousand bullets per minute tearing through the ranks of an advancing regiment or two! Men go down like grass before the mower. None but the bravest can go forward. It takes real men to face such tornadoes of destruction. Artillery is almost useless against these sunken trenches. At a thousand yards you can only guess where the trench is, for remember that modern rifles make no smoke. Moreover, at a thousand yards the artillery will lose more men, picked off by the hidden enemy in the trenches, than those same men in trenches will lose from the enemy's artillery fire. Truly the war that our fathers knew, thirty-five years ago, was child's play compared with the modern attacks of infantry against other infantry fortified in these sunken trenches.

The textbooks that military men study say that such attacks against fortified infantry are impossible except where the assaulting party outnumbers the defenders many times over. And General Linares, who commanded at Santiago, and who planned and supervised the construction of the defenses all the way from Daiquiri to Santiago, is a recognized European authority on fortifications. Hearing a chuckle, I turned around and saw my friend, the major-correspondent, also inspecting the trench.

"I'm thinking," he explained, "how lucky we were that the Spaniards lost their sand when they saw our gunboats moving in Wednesday morning. There were five hundred men garrisoned here, and the commandant was writing a letter to Linares, informing the general that he had sufficient force to frustrate the landing of the American army. Of a sudden one of his officers informed him that the American fleet was approaching. He came out, took one startled look at the great fleet, and set his troops in motion for the interior. The letter was found by one of our soldiers."

"But couldn't our navy have shelled them out of the trenches?"

"The navy did shell," replied the Major. "Have you seen any spot where it looked as if a shell struck the trench? Can you shoot a revolver?"

"Fairly well," I answered.

"Then get a half-inch rope. Lay it on the ground, in a drill a half an inch deep, so that the uppermost strands of the rope are just level with the ground. Next step off a hundred yards and try to hit that rope. Keep count of how many times you hit in a week's practice. That will give you some idea of how difficult it would be for the Navy to shell brave men out of these trenches. If they had been held by five hundred of the enemy as brave and of as accurate marksmanship as our own troops," added the major, solemnly, "Shafter's army of 15,000 men would still be out on the water, except those who were moving in it. We couldn't have landed troops as fast as the Spaniards could have shot them. My amazement increases every time I think of the Spaniards taking to their heels without waiting to fire a shot from this strong position."

Pretty soon we went over to take a look at a blockhouse which had escaped demolition by the navy's guns. Now, this blockhouse, which the Spaniards call a *fortina*, is another grim death-trap for infantry assailants. Few of these *fortinas* are more than a dozen feet square. First of all there is the cellar, well protected by earth hard banked up. The house is built of heavy timbers, and having double walls. Between the inner and outer walls the space of six or eight inches is filled with finely broken stone. At the ground line is the firing aperture for the soldiers in the basement. There is another firing aperture, about five feet from the ground, for the soldiers who stand on the floor of the *fortina*. Each aperture is about three inches high, and runs all around the *fortina*, save where the upright supports interfere. Fifty good men in a *fortina* can hold off a regiment of infantry, for the men in the *fortina* can do about all of killing. But there is this difference between the trench and the *fortina*—the latter offers a fair mark for field artillery. Inspecting these works of defense and knowing that similar ones existed along the whole length of the road to Santiago, we began to have visions of a bloody campaign ahead. We were convinced, later on, that with these magnificent fortifications, the Spaniards, had they been up to their own estimate as fighters, could have made it cost us fifty thousand men to get within sight of Santiago. One well-informed military officer put the case more strongly when he said:

"If Spain had had real soldiers here she could have made our advance cost us a man for every foot."

There came a time—it came soon, too—when the base of supplies was changed to Siboney, four miles down the coast, or eight over the mountain trails. It contained, probably, a hundred and fifty houses. We went down there on Monday, on one of the smaller transports, the *Cumberland*, our friend, the major-correspondent, arranging for our transportation. Several of us, instead of putting up tents at Siboney, took quarters in an abandoned house—an infected "shack". Later, when the yellow fever came, some of the men in our house were among the earliest to sicken with it.

But we were in Cuba to see a fight. We talked fight, thought fight, wrote of fight. War and its problems were our mental food. We longed for the first battle. It was not long before we were gratified. We marched to the front, saw a whole day of terrific fighting, and all the horrors and other incidents of war as waged in the progressive year of 1898.

# Chapter VI
# In Camp at Siboney

Siboney is a name that will be long remembered by all who had any share in the invasion of Santiago province. This little sea-coast village had a population, in the normal times, of possibly a thousand souls. It was the best base of supplies at hand for the campaign against the city of Santiago. Here the remainder of Shafter's Army Corps debarked; here the commissary, quartermaster's and ordnance departments made their headquarters, and here, also, the big hospital was established.

Surrounded by hills, which hemmed it close down to the beach, lay Siboney. It is correct to use the past tense, for subsequently every house in the wretched place was burned. Near the beach was a cluster of a dozen or so squalid houses, in the midst of which towered a sawmill and a storehouse. The former was promptly taken possession of by the engineers; the latter was just the kind of building to suit the commissary. West of these buildings flowed a sluggish creek, emptying into a stagnant pond, which, though it had no outlet, was separated from the ocean by only a few yards of sandy beach. All around this creek were swamp and slime—an ideal soil for breeding malaria and fever germs. The Spanish soldiers had never dug the short ditch that would have brought the restless, salubrious ocean into this foul basin of disease culture. Perhaps we should not be too hard upon the negligent Spaniards; it was well on in July, after the fever had started, when our own engineers found time to make the short cut between swamp and ocean.

From the creek ran a dirty street in a general southwesterly direction. This street bordered upon the railroad track, which ran along the shore to Aguadores, and thence to the outskirts of Santiago. The street, which ended at the railroad round-house, was flanked on the side furthest from the bay by a row of whitewashed wooden houses. First of all came a roomy, high-stooped affair which, in happier times, had been the only store of the village. When our party reached Siboney it was being used as a residence for army surgeons and medical storehouse—this, despite the fact that it had been reported to the medical officers as one of the worst yellow fever infected houses in the village. And next to this high-stooped building was a long, shed-like structure in which was located the first army hospital. Here, upon blankets on the ingrained dirt of the floor, lay several Rough Riders wounded in the fight at Las Guasimas. There were also several cases of sickness being treated here. It was a foul, wretched place, though, under the doctors' orders, the men of the hospital corps had toned it down to some semblance of cleanliness. Just beyond the hospital was an open shed. There the Spanish soldiers, when they were masters of the town, had done their cooking. Here also was the faucet and running water which constituted the "public works" of Siboney. Then, after a stretch of open field, came the four-room shack which several of us seized upon as a temporary home. We were warned that our building had once been a Spanish military hospital and was doubtless infected with yellow fever.

"Is it worse infected than any other building, tree, bush, pebble or cocoanut husk in town?" I asked one of the surgeons.

"Probably not," he replied, with a shrug. "The whole place must be alive with germs."

So we took possession of the shack which was, at all events, drier than our tents could have been during the daily rains of the season. Just beyond us were two small buildings appropriated by two New York newspapers; then the office of the signal corps. Next came the camp of the engineers, and between them and the roundhouse lay the field in which, subsequently, the numerous tents of the hospital were erected. Back of our street ran another which extended much further, and along this second thoroughfare were most of the houses of the town—mean, low, squalid shacks for the most part. There were a few that were somewhat roomy, notably the Red Cross Hospital, the Cuban hospital, and General Bates' headquarters. In all Siboney there had never been a church, but one store, already referred to, and no structure which, judged by any externals, had ever been a public building. But blockhouses! They were everywhere in the twon and guarding every approach to it. Evidently the Spanish soldiers had a mania for building these blockhouses. Had they shown the same zeal in defending them, our advance upon

Santiago would have been slow and costly in human lives.

Certainly our base of supplies was well defended at this time. There were two brigades of troops—General Bates', comprising the Third and Twentieth U.S. Infantry, and General Duffield's, made up of the Thirty-third and Thirty-fourth Michigan volunteers. There was need of these soldiers, for down on the beach, in addition to the vast ordnance stores piling up, were commissary stores roughly estimated at a value of a million dollars. At a little distance back from the beach was the commissary store itself—a most wonderful kind of emporium where everything was sold at cost to officers and correspondents. The enlisted men didn't have to pay for their food supplies, which were drawn on requisition for them by regimental officers. I frequently run across people up here in the United States who imagine that our commissary officers were able to "line their pockets" with the profits of sharp bargain driving. Those who think anything of the sort have confounded the modern commissary with the old-time sutler. The commissary men sell at prices established by the government, and the price of each article is its cost at wholesale, without the cost of transportation added. The cash received from officers and civilians is turned over to the Government; there is no profit for anyone, unless it be for the buyer. As for the commissary supplies, they were undeniably good enough for the stomachs of any men living an active, outdoor life, consisting mainly of hard-tack, bacon, canned meats, fruits and vegetables, soups, coffee, tea, sugar, flour and baking powder. The canned fruits and soups, however, were not issued to enlisted men, unless by surgeon's order; these belonged for "officers' stores." Correspondents were privileged to buy them, and our mess, with the addition of some supplies brought from the United States, fared as well as we could have wished to. So did all the officers and men at Siboney. Out at the front it was a different matter. There men had a more monotonous fare. Often they were fortunate if they had any whatever. Tobacco, especially, was scarce. One rough rider, in camp a few miles from Siboney, paid ten dollars for half a pound of an inferior kind. Another soldier, a regular, coveted a half hand of chewing tobacco of which a comrade was the fortunate possessor.

"What'll you take for it, Jack?" asked the man who hadn't of the man who had.

"Don't want to sell it," replied Jack, taking a tantalizingly big chew from the piece. The man who hadn't watched the ecstatic motion of the luckier one's jaws until he could endure it no longer.

"See here, Jack, I'll give you all the money I've got in my clothes for that piece of plug."

Jack stopped chewing and looked reflective. The would-be buyer was known in the regiment to be a thrifty fellow.

"I'll do it," finally decided the owner of the tobacco.

He handed the plug over, and its new owner, in turn, went through all his pockets, turning out twenty-seven dollars and some odd change.

"It that isn't enough, Jack," suggested the buyer, go to my haversack—handle it careful—and you'll find seven hundred dollars there. Help yourself to what you think is right."

But Jack, be it said to his honor, was content, even in those days of severe deprivation, to accept twenty-seven dollars as a fair equivalent for twenty cents' worth of tobacco. I mention the scarcity of this article merely as indicating how difficult it was to get a good many needed things to our men at the front. And tobacco is undeniably a necessity to the soldier in the field. Later on, in the evening after the second day's fighting, General Shafter was quoted as saying that he would give "the boys" as easy a time as possible until all had been provided with at least one good, "square" meal and a smoke. There was an abundance of food piled up at the commissary; there were hundreds of tons of it never unloaded from the ships. Had there been mule wagons enough no soldier at the front need have gone hungry, as many entire commands did do at times. Whether the engineers could have rendered the roads more easily passable for what wagons there were is a question for civil engineers to decide. Wherever the blame lay will doubtless be found this winter by Congressmen of an inquiring turn of mind. Only this much is certain, as being easily ascertainable—that had ammunition been as slightingly served as was food on the two days of great fighting, defeat would have resulted.

In the meantime the Government post-office was back at Daiquiri, where the troops first landed. Why? The same old story, "lack of transportation facilities." There was all the post-office paraphernalia at Daiquiri, all of the six postal employees and their baggage—not to mention the thousands of letters for which homesick soldiers were clamouring. A soldier who wanted to post a letter home and who secured leave to come into Siboney for that purpose, was told that he must tramp eight miles further over the mountains. Yet folks at home wondered why they didn't hear promptly from their soldier boys. Postmaster Eben Brewer came wearily over that Daiquiri trail, not one but many times. He was an energetic official, constantly on the trail of transportation. All the while soldiers were tramping about Siboney, inquiring where letters could be for the mail, I would act as his deputy at Siboney without pay. He caught at the idea and gladly consented. And so I became soldiers' postmaster at Siboney. The duties were not onerous, but they took a good deal of my time. The post-office outfit was simple, consisting of a hard-tack box just inside the door, and a paper pasted up inside on which was written:

"MAIL YOUR LETTERS HERE."

Siboney will never do as large a mail business again. In the first two days nearly eight thousand letters were left with me. As I sat at my table writing, soldiers passed in, deposited their letters, and filed out. Few of them asked any questions; none asked foolish ones. An additional placard informed them that only out-going mail was handled here and, further, that the unsalaried deputy had no idea when the next mail would leave for the United States. Few of the soldiers had stamps. Nearly all had provided themselves, but the little pink affairs stuck together in that hot, humid climate, and so became useless. It was required that every letter should be stamped or franked. Not one in a hundred was stamped. The franking consisted in writing "Soldier's Letter" on the envelope. Below this inscription was needed the signature, rank and regiment of some commissioned officer. At first I explained this to each soldier who entered with mail. He would promptly depart in search of an officer. Soon I found that such frequent interruption for explanation would seriously interfere with my own work. After that, I devoted a leisure portion of each day to sorting over the letters, piling aside all that had not been franked. With these in my hands I would go outside and hail the first officer who passed. It often took my victim an hour or two to frank all the letters I handed him. It is a pleasant memory picture in these after days, that of a commissioned officer—and sometimes two or three—sitting on the porch of our shack, writing away for dear life on the ends of envelopes. Only two officers, out of all that I asked, declined to frank letters, and they explained that they were on duty of an imperative character. There was brotherhood in Siboney between all men, of whatever rank, who had friends at home to read letters. The faces of the envelopes of the soldiers' letters afforded a profitable field for study and speculation, 85 per cent of the mail being addressed "Mrs" or "Miss" Somebody. Most of the men who stay at home must have to read second-hand letters.

# Chapter VII
# The Longing for Battle

Now all of this life was very interesting, but it was not war. We correspondents went to Cuba to see fighting, and fighting we had to have. There was even some little talk of organizing ourselves into a battalion and going out to seek the enemy, without waiting for the army. But it was pointed out that there might be more or less danger attending such an expedition, and so the notion never got beyond the stage of smoke talk during the periods of comfort and content just after meals. Some of the correspondents were already out at the front, living with the troops night and day. Others of us, whose work required us to keep near what mail communication there was, remained at Siboney, but we had the assurances of military authorities that we should receive a hint in ample season. Nor was that promise broken.

The hint came on the afternoon of Thursday, June 30. There was to be a fight on the morrow, if the Spaniards could be found, and on the latter score very little doubt was felt. Then there was a scurrying through camp. Within an hour a dozen correspondents had left, and were trudging over the hills. By dark another dozen had departed.

"General Bates' Brigade will pull out of here at nine to-night. They are promised a good place in tomorrow's fight."

That was another tip, quickly verified. I had heard of the terrors of the mountain trail ahead of us. Frequently a few miles of it had worn out an able-bodied man. Frankly, I dreaded it, but the tramp had to be made, since there were no seats to be had on wagons, and saddle horses were simply out of the question.

"Suppose we wait and go with General Bates," I suggested to Messrs Maxwell and Ewan, two of my fellow correspondents. "If we go with the troops we're sure to see the fight, and it ought to be easier traveling if we have a whole brigade to set the pace for us." My comrades agreeing, the next thing in order was to get into "rough clothes". These consisted of canvas trousers and leggings, flannel shirts and sombreros. Next each of us did up a pair of blankets and a poncho into a roll, to be worn over the shoulder and passing down over the other hip. With canteen, cartridge belt and pistol the outfit for the field was complete.

Rations were to be stowed at the last moment. Then we began to think of our belongings in the shack. Some of them we did not care to lose, and the reputation for honesty of the Cubans thereabouts—well, we in Siboney always summed it up by saying, "What they can't get at is safe."

With that thought uppermost, I hurried up the dirty street to where the new field hospital had been established. Here, indeed, were grim hints of what was coming. Soldiers were busy putting up hospital tents, three in a row, and row after row—a white canvas village capable of sheltering battalions of shattered men. Surgeon Major Lagarde of the United States

Army was now in charge, a humane, energetic, kindly man, capable apparently of living without sleep. He heard what I wanted, and immediately replied: "Bring your things right up here and put them in my tent. If we become crowded, I may have to put them out in the rain, but my own things shall go first."

There I took my more valuable effects, including a typewriter. Here, also, with the willing help of soldiers, I carried the boxes of mail that had been accumulating in our shack. Next our trio hurried to the quarters of General Bates. He gave us unreserved permission to accompany his brigade wherever it went. Then back to supper! We were happy as youngsters who have been promised an evening at the circus. If soldiers are elated at the prospect of a fight, war correspondents are no less so. After a period of fightless inactivity the prospect of a battle is absolutely cheering. There was a chance, of course, that one or all of us would fail to come back. Honestly, I don't think we thought of that.

"Going out to-night, boys?" called a mounted officer as he rode by our open-air table at the end of the shack.

"Make no mistake about it!"

"You're doing the right thing, then. Eat all you can before you go. There's precious little at the front."

"Come and help us?"

He needed no second invitation, but springing out of the saddle, tied his horse to the corner post of the shack's porch and came toward us.

"It's decidedly kind of you," he murmured, but we

dissented. Army men are the most hospitable in the world, on their own health, as we had already discovered in trips through camps. Our guest explained to us, as we ate hurriedly, that he had ridden in with an urgent order, and was due back at the front at the earliest possible moment. All was motion out there. Everything betokened the start of a lively fight at daylight.

"Is there any chance of taking Santiago tomorrow?" I asked.

"Only heaven and the generals know," he replied, with a shrug. "Gentlemen, I shall finish this meal in the saddle if you don't mind. But I thank you from the bottom of my boots, for the famine extended way down there before I saw you."

With a handful of food, he sprang into the saddle and galloped off. His very haste made us the more eager to start, but as yet it was only half-past seven. In what was, for us, heavy marching order, we sat down and smoked at a point where we could keep watch of the only road by which Bates' men could leave Siboney.

Across the little bay, on the slope behind a ruined Spanish fort of seventeenth century style, blazed the campfires of a battalion of Michigan Volunteers. Down on the beach itself, where the lights moved to and fro, men were busy handling stores of subsistence and ammunition. A train of mules, each burdened with two cases of cartridges, toiled up the steep road over which we would soon be journeying. In the bay and out to sea lay a score of transports, lighted up and live-looking. In and out among them moved three or four of the lesser fighting craft of the navy. From somewhere among the campfires on the distant slopes came the sound of a bugle call, and immediately after it a long-winded response from a trumpeter belong to the Cuban force in the blockhouse at the top of the long hill. Wagons went creaking by, on their way to the lower road, which joined the upper one further on. An ambulance passed, with its load of stretchers and supply chests.

The town was full of dark-skinned Cubans, carrying rusty guns and jagged machetes, gesticulating freely and describing volubly what they would do to the Spaniards on the morrow. It was a picture of war that interested us more than anything we had seen since the bombardment of Daiquiri.

# Chapter VIII
# The Ascent of "Awful Hill"

"Here they come!" And here they came indeed - first General Bates and his staff, all mounted, and then the head of the third Infantry. As far back as we could see down the dark street were moving men—Uncle Sam's men on the march, and bent on no playful errand! Someone else must have been eager in Siboney that night, for the column started fifteen minutes ahead of the appointed time. No more splendid-looking lot of soldiers could be found than these men of the Third and Twentieth. They were regulars—men carefully picked, in times of peace, for physique and intelligence. On they came in a column of fours with swinging, rhythmic, tireless tread. They had risen at 5.30 that morning, had performed the full day of routine camp work and were yet fresh for mountain climbing! There was nothing about them that savored of parade. Their apparel of flannel shirt and rough old trousers suggested the working man, with only the leggings to give a military aspect to their clothing. On their heads were *sombreros*, already much the worse for their steady use as camp pillows at night. Each man carried a heavy roll slung over one shoulder; the ammunition belts, with full supply of cartridges, weighed several pounds apiece. A canteen, full of water, added four pounds to the burden. Guns were carried any way that was comfortable. Here and there was a man who shouldered a pick, another a shovel—tools that were intended for the morrow for digging trenches in which the living might seek shelter from the enemy's bullets—trenches in which the dead would find communistic graves of glory and honor. Yet on they came, shifting packs, smoking pipes and chatting on every subject except the chances of the morrow. To the regular army soldier fighting is a trade. Time enough to think about it when the work begins.

At the base of the hill they fell into columns of twos. Up they went, striking a gradual ascent at first, then a road that became steeper with every second step. How we felt the tortures of that climb! By "we" I don't mean to include the soldiers. They took it as a matter of course, and found it only a little fatiguing. But to the uninitiated noncombatants it was "Awful Hill". We reached the top at last. Thank God! Forward and right on went the sturdy line. Gradually we caught our second wind. We had fallen in at the head of the Twentieth, but now found ourselves walking with three officers of the Third. One of them fell back at my side, saying:

"My name is Houle." I told him my own name, and we shook hands. That is all the ceremony there is to introduction in the field. He introduced me to Captain French and Dr Bragg. In return, I presented Messrs Maxwell and Ewan. It was only a chance meeting, but we were quickly made to feel that we had fallen among friends. We asked them many questions about the lay of the land and the prospects of the morrow, all of which they answered as fully as they could.

Then they questioned us about a practical topic—the amount of provisions we had taken with us.

Doffing my *sombrero*, I displayed the five squares of hard-tack resting inside. My two comrades were no better supplied. Then Dr Bragg inforned us that, being entitled to ride, he had chosen to walk, and had packed his horse with things edible. "If you find yourselves short of food over yonder," he added, "hunt up Dr Bragg of the Third Infantry." Then we remembered with pleasure our slight hospitality to one of his brother officers earlier in the evening.

And now the men marching ahead began to slow up, the files of two closing the former intervals before they halted, with much the same effect as a long freight train coming to a stop.

It is a halt, and surely, if the men are human, they need it! They are reeking with perspiration. It is a wonder their bodies do not give off dense exhalations of steam.

"A soldier's first duty," says Lieutenant Houle, "is to make himself as comfortable as possible." He exemplifies it by casting off roll, haversack and canteen. The roll he utilizes as a seat; the canteen he applies to his lips, swallowing only a few spoonfuls of water. He, the captain and the doctor, light cigarettes; we prefer our pipes. It is so good to have a rest that we do not spoil the effect by talking much. Many of the soldiers down the line ahead of us are short of tobacco. I supply several of them and receive quiet but hearty thanks.

There is time for only a short smoke, and then we are going forward again, starting so quickly that we are obliged to adjust our packs as we march. In spots the road is rock-strewn, the jagged, flinty fragments making themselves felt through the thickest soles of leather. Then we come to muddy stretches where we sink in half-way up to our knees. We are proceeding in single file by this time, for the road is too narrow for men to march side by side.

"Road" is a term of convenience; it doesn't describe the miserable trail on which we are traveling. "The King's Road" some fanciful Spanish official had christened it long ago. If the little King of the small brown men could have seen that road he would have blushed. After perhaps a half an hour of further marching another blessed halt occurs. It takes considerable time for the news to travel to the last man of all. A brigade in single file is long drawn out. But we sit down on our rolls as soon as the word reaches us. And now, though the moon's light is struggling through the dense foliage overhead, and the few stars that we can see look big and bright, there is a steady, constant plashing of water drops on jungle and ground. Raining? That is the first belief, but a wrong one. It is merely the heavy dew, which settling on the leaves, runs down to their points, the moisture gathering in volume until the drops fall. It might as well be raining, for this audible, visible dew doesn't need long to drench its victims.

On again! It must be five minutes after the head of the line starts before the same motion is communicated to the men who bring up the rear. Except for the underfoot portion it is a beautiful country through which we are passing. The moonlight, of which we get occasional glimpses, shines with a wonderful lustre on the scores of different trees. On either side of the road there is thick jungle. An army marching along this course cannot have flankers, for men could not make anything like a mile an hour through the jungle.

"What would happen if Spaniards were lying in ambush through the jungle along this road?" I ask of Captain French and Lieutenant Houle.

"If their marksmanship were anything like good," comes the simple answer, "They would swiftly annihilate us."

And yet there are miles and miles of this road, along which the army had been marching to the front for days. One cannot help thinking that the Spanish commanders are poor soldiers when they have permitted this with only the solitary ambuscade episode of Las Guasimas. There is even opportunity for them to attack this last brigade of all, for the troops already out at the front cannot be so widely spread as to shut off all sallies out of Santiago.

If we are not attacked on this night is it not another proof of Spanish incompetence in fighting? It was supposed, of course, in advance, that the Cubans, used to penetrating the jungles, would be constantly on our flanks to nose out any lurking enemy but the less said about the Cubans the better. There is a slowing up ahead that looks like a halt, but it isn't.

Those ahead of us have reached a stream that has to be forded. We come to it, and in we go. It is only a few yards across, and out we come on the other side with wet legs. Life is not quite the same after fording a stream. The feet are wet and go sloshing about in shoes that seem suddenly too large.

Somehow the sand gets in above the soles, and we are treading on grit the rest of the way until—we come to another stream, and our discomfort is intensified. And all the time we are so hot and moist that clothing seems but a sponge of warm water. Yet when, in more open intervals of country, we see vistas of moon-lit tropical forest, hear the musical calls of night birds and smell the fragrance of rich, damp, tropical flowers, there is compensation for personal irritations. Truly a night march, with just a hint of suspense about possible ambuscade, is the romance of campaigning in the tropics. It is worth a dozen day marches!

At last we pass a goodly cluster of little, low "dog tents". Under these are sleeping a regiment of infantrymen. We are nearing the front, then. And next we pass a slumbering battery, and then another infantry regiment. We are in the thick of the troops now. They are posted all along the road, and the romance of war and night marching grows tense. As we pass sentinels standing by the roadside we ask, "What regiment?" and the answer is always promptly forthcoming. So we gain some idea of the disposition of Shafter's corps. Sentinels look wistfully after us going far on to the front. They imagine Bates' men are going to be in the advance pack the morrow, and envy us our good luck.

# Chapter IX
# The Night Before the Battle

And then there comes a halt. We have reached another camp. All about us we see regimental clusters of dog tents, and over there to the northward a small, very small village of much larger wall tents. That is the headquarters of General Shafter and his staff. They are sleeping soundly, most of them, against the fatigues of the morrow, for it is now a half an hour before midnight. Soon we are moving off the road and into the broad field, and through the long grass that is up to our thighs. A bustling staff officer on horseback charges through the field, shouting words here and there. The men halt, in regular company lines, and almost instantly the little rows of white dog tents are up. It is like magic, for with the bewildering appearance of the tents has come the disappearance of the men. They have crawled in under their tents and are already slumbering.

They sleep two in a tent, each man having carried half of that tent in his roll. A staff officer shouts out the location of the nearest water, and adds the information that the first call to reveille will sound at 4.45 am. We of the pencils have no tents, neither have Captain French nor Lieutenant Houle. Therefore we tread down the grass to some near approach to flatness, and spread our *ponchos*.

"Here, you'll have to get out of there! There's a regiment going to march in there in a minute," cries the ubiquitous staff officer, and that sends us down to the head of the line of H company.

"Sorry, gentlemen, but you'll have to move away from there," proclaims the staff officer, reappearing after two minutes. This man with a mania for making people "move on" is as troublesome as the farce-comedy policeman. Nevertheless, three correspondents get wearily up from their *ponchos*, but Captain French calls out: "Will you oblige me by chasing someone else? I'm with my company."

"Oh, I beg your pardon, captain." This is the last we see of the staff officer, and we settle down again. Now for field bed-making. The *poncho*, when spread out, is simply a rubber blanket. On this is placed a pair of woolen blankets, in which the intending sleeper rolls himself up. Dr Bragg has disappeared. Maxwell and Ewan go promptly to sleep, but Captain French, Lieutenant Houle and writer sit down on the ready-made beds to first eat a bit and then enjoy a smoke. The talk ranges back to the United States, and soon settles upon that inevitable topic in the field—wives and youngsters. Mr Houle, who has no personal interest in this talk, proves a good listener.

There are others abroad, and presently they come nearer. Then a low-voiced invitation to "step out here," and the canteen that is displayed does not contain water. A swallow of rum is urged as an excellent thing to ward off malaria and chill. It seems absurd to speak of chill when summering in the tropics but now the dew is like fine rain. It is 1.30 am when we roll ourselves up in our blankets, with *sombreros* for pillows. Mr Houle, who has been provided by a thoughtful Government with an abdominal band, discovers that its true use is as a nightcap in this climate where the dew pours! Before falling asleep I ask Captain French to make sure that I am not left behind in the morning through oversleeping. He readily agrees. I add that I am a heavy sleeper and may require rough treatment.

"If you can sleep over the rousing I'll give you, you're a miracle," is his prompt response, and I go to sleep.

Who is that fiend who doesn't know better than to practice on a cornet where others are trying to sleep? He ought to be court-martialed! He ought to be—but it's the bugler, and there is a good deal of red in the sky of dawn. It is twenty-five minutes past four. First call to reveille is twenty minutes earlier than it had been promised. Lieutenant Houle is sitting up on his blanket. I imitate him, and find Maxwell and Ewan blinking sleepily about them. But Captain French slumbers deeply. We can't see Santiago but the sky in that direction is a mass of dark red clouds and vivid reds.

"Santiago is on fire!" cries one of the soldiers whom the bugle has brought out of a dog tent. He has made a mistake, but it is pardonable, for this glorious sky effect of a Cuban sunrise looks wonderfully like a distant view of a conflagration.

"*Français!*" sounds the deep, heavy voice of Houle, as the lieutenant rests a rousing hand on the shoulder of his superior officer. The captain sleeps on, until Houle, tiring of homeopathic means, picks up the company's commander, blanket and all, and runs about, jolting the sleeper until he opens his eyes and slides to his feet. It is very likely a bit of dramatic frolic, but I say things under my breath when I try my camera and find that the lens shutter won't work. My teeth began to chatter, for clothes and blankets were wet through by the drenching dew.

It looks as if I were afraid of the fight that is coming, and I make some laughing remark of the kind, but Lieutenant Houle, with a smile, goes off and gets me some more of that rum. It stops the chattering, and the sun's coming up dispels the last chill. Little fires have been kindled all over the field. There is a smell of coffee in the air, and a sizzling of bacon. Breakfast is on, quicker than any housewife can get it. I am urged to dip into other men's frying pans, but they have none too much food on which to do a day's deadly work, and I am to be only an idler. So I decline and munch two of my hardtack. I place my cup beside me, intending to fill it from the canteen, but a soldier stealthily gets possession of it and returns it full of piping hot coffee. I suspect that he is one of the men who had some of my tobacco the night before.

The tents have been struck and made up into rolls. Maxwell and Ewan have started off by themselves. I prefer to keep with the troops. Now the bugler, whom a half an hour ago I would have had court-martialed, is at it again. The two regiments are forming. There is roll call and a counting of fours. Before we are expecting it, commands ring out, men wheel to the left by fours and head for the road. It is the morning of the first of July, and we are going into battle.

*"There is a smell of coffee in the air and a sizzling of bacon."*

# Chapter X
# With Bates' Brigade

When we swung out from the campfield into the road on the morning of July 1, there were few men in Bates' Brigade who had any idea where we were to go that day, or what part we were to play. Certainly I was not one of those who knew, nor did any of the officers with whom I chatted as we moved along up the road in the cool of the morning.

Some had heard that we were to move into position on the left of the line. This promised well for if, as some expected, we were to capture Santiago that day, the left of the line would place us among the first to enter the captured city. But only a few hundred yards had we gone when we halted. While lounging by the roadside we were passed by a few fugitives— old men, women and young children—who had gotten out of the hunger-ridden city of Santiago, and who were now on their way to Siboney to taste of our famed American canned meats and hard-tack. After a few minutes the order came to move forward. Boom! came the sound of a gun from El Poso, which told us what we had not positively known before—that the day's battle was on in earnest. By the time that we had gone something more than a mile we were wheeled into a field, ranks broken and arms stacked. This did not look like hurrying into the fight, but those who were conducting the day's operations knew better than we where the brigade would be of most service. And right good use did many of these soldiers make of their opportunity by supplementing the short rest of the night by going to sleep now.

"There goes the balloon!" shouted someone, and in an instant apathy changed to keen interest, and those of us who were asleep woke up. Off to the eastward or southeast, appeared the round, yellow bag above the treetops, glistening in the morning sun as if it had risen out of the dew. This was one of the fantastic military chimeras of the military authorities. It seemed as if the balloon had been but a few moments over the treetops when it began to descend. Back there in Bates' Brigade we surmised, though we did not know, that the enemy's marksmen had proven themselves able to hit the big yellow bag. It went down quickly enough, and after a while the second balloon went up—went up a little higher and stayed a little longer—before it too came sinking down to earth. The military balloon, it was evident even from our position at the rear, had proven a ludicrous failure. We laughed about it then, for none of us knew at that time that the balloon had been sent up at a point that utterly betrayed the location of our own advancing men, resulting in a considerable loss of American life.

It would be interesting to know just who was mainly responsible for the crime of sending up the balloon at that point. The Spanish made excellent use of the information our balloons furnished them, and sent showers of hissing Mauser bullets into the grass and clumps of chaparral around the anchor lines of those preposterous gasbags, striking down men right and left.

Not realizing the needless tragedies attached to this spectacular bit of aeronautics, we back there at the rear stretched ourselves on *ponchos* in the shade and again made up for some of the sleep lost the night before. I had already made up my mind not to be impatient for a sight of the fight, but to await the turn of events; so, instead of hurrying forward on my own account, I stretched myself out between Captain French and Lieutenant Houle, and we all three slept until the shifting sun found us out and chased us to the shade of another tree. Just as we were starting there was a stentorian shout of:

"H Company, come and get it!"

It is in these words that the readiness of a meal is announced in camp. There was a wild stampede toward a patch of long grass from which the yell came—then rough, hearty guffaws. It was all a hoax. There was nothing to "come and get", for almost the last had been eaten at early breakfast. These men were really hungry enough to enjoy a good meal, but they were regulars, and a regular in a campaign is apt to scorn a man who cannot go two or three days without eating. We found the shade, prepared to enjoy it, when the shrill notes of bugles called every man to his post. Orders rang out briskly now, and men moved with alacrity. In the time that an ordinary man would require to put on his shoes and lace them up, these two regiments had fallen in and were heading for the road.

The real thing now! No more short, leisurely marches, with long halts! The mounted general and his mounted staff up at the head of the column set a pace that was hard to follow. The man who was to stay in that column must lift up his feet and put them down quickly, with a long stride between. It had now reached the hottest part of the morning, and the gait soon produced suffering. In a few moments we were at a ford. Someone who had gone before us had taken the trouble to roll big stones into the shallow stream, the succession of these forming a sort of a bridge. But it was slow work for a long line of men to pass over these stones, and many tried to find other ways.

It was at best slow work, and to get some twenty companies over in this fashion would consume a good deal of valuable time.

"Don't bother about wet feet!" shouted Captain French, himself wading in where the water was deepest, an example which hurried the men through the creek and up the opposite bank. Then on again, in Indian file, with boots heavier and feeling as if full of pebbles. A long, up-hill toil on a steep mountain trail. More fording and a constant succession of steep hills. I remember thinking it marvelous that men could make mile after mile of this kind of journeying at such a gait, and without halts, to say nothing of fighting at the end. But the pacemaker continued inexorable, and we had to follow somehow at a pace that was half walk and half run.

After two miles of this sort of thing I saw a soldier drop out and sink to a seat by the roadside. As we passed him, I saw that his face was as red as a lobster's shell and, though he had passed the enlistment surgeon as a perfectly sound man, I could see his heart beating now under his shirt. He took a long pull at the canteen, gasping as he removed it from his lips.

"Come as soon as you can," called an officer in passing, and the poor fellow nodded his head, an answer that saved breath.

It was not long before another dropped out, and then another, at every few rods. I was suffering myself, stopping now and then for a pull at the warm water in my canteen, then hurrying on again. There was not a man in the line who would not have given a good part of his month's pay for a ten minute halt. It came not, and the regular soldier has too much *esprit de corps* to fall by the wayside while there remains any possibility of his going onward.

At the end of three miles of this sort of thing I knew something about the sufferings of a forced march in the tropics. Twenty men had dropped out by this time. I would have given much to fall out and sink down beside the last one. Lieutenant Houle, noting my condition, advised me to do so. But pride made me shake my head. Back in Tampa the soldiers had settled it for themselves that the correspondents would be miles to the rear when the fighting was going on. They chaffed us about it in advance and I, for one, was determined to stagger on and into the fight somehow. So, bent nearly double under my pack, streaming perspiration at every step, panting, gasping and with a sharp pain beginning in my side, I kept on. For a little part of the way Lieutenant

Houle took hold of my arm to help me, but I knew he would have plenty of need of all his reserve strength that day, and shook free of him, following in his footsteps.

Despite myself, I began to lag. Sergeant Hart, of H Company, was now treading on my heels. I spurted ahead but two or three times during the next five minutes I found his relentless boots grinding against mine.

"I you can't keep the gait, why don't you fall out like the others?" he growled at last, exasperated. Lieutenant Houle, hearing, fell back beside me, without a word, and I struggled to keep step with him. "Why don't you fall out, and come on with the second battalion?" he suggested, after a while. "They're three or four minutes behind us." But I felt that if I once sat down on the seductive grass that bordered the road it would be long before I could summon up the strength to go on again. Thank God for the halt that came! But, no; before there was time to sit down the line ahead started again; it was only a momentary slackening. All along the men of H Company had been requesting permission to discard their packs, but Captain French, knowing how necessary the packs would be later on, had refused. During this brief semi-halt, however, he saw the weakening condition of his men, and ordered them to stack their packs in a company pile. We were in motion before the last discarded roll fell on the pile. We were climbing the last long slant to the ridge from which Capron's battery had been thundering against El Caney earlier in the morning. Now the guns were still, but from the hills of El Caney, long before we came in sight of them, we could hear the sharp, incessant rattle of rifle fire. What did the battle sound like at this distance? The most persistent stay-at-home body can form an accurate idea. Imagine several hundred boys in a village, each with an inexhaustible supply of cannon-crackers, setting them off unceasingly, whole packs at a time. There you have the sound, as perfect as the original itself. Imaging this pop-pop-popping of cannon-crackers from daylight to dark, with never a let-up to light punk or go after more crackers, and you will have a clear perception of the audible portion of what the Spaniards, with our very able assistance, were doing at El Caney on the First of July.

"There's a dickens of a fight going on over there," said Lieutenant Houle.

He looked interested, but not excited. His thoughts were certainly more busy with the men of H Company than with the yet distant battle. He and Captain French both turned frequently to see how the men were standing the stiff pace. They were straggling a trifle—surely they could not be blamed for it, for they were making the stiffest march performed by any of our troops that day.

"Sergeant," called Captain French, "pass word back to close up the line."

Sergeant Hart, though a splendid physical specimen of a man, was suffering from both heat and fatigue. To go back along that line of some forty or fifty men, closing up the gaps and then running back to his own place at the head of the company, was no light task on that steep hillside. Yet without a frown, or a trace of the impatient look that a man less a soldier would have given under the circumstances, he saluted, turned and started back. It seemed too bad for, his order carried out, the run back to the head of the company line was sure to land him there gasping. But Lieutenant Houle, seeing him start, called after him:

"Pass the word back, sergeant. Don't go back."

Then relief showed in the sergeant's face, as he came back, straightened up, saluted and sent back word that soon closed up the gaps. He was a soldier all the way through and non-commissioned officers like him, by their own unhesitating obedience and ungrumbling readiness for whatever came, were as valuable in the campaign as our generals.

It is always interesting to the uninitiated to think how soldiers feel who are going into battle. Are they afraid? Do they feel queer sensations—nausea? Fright? An inclination to head about and run back? Do they think of home, and wish, by all the gods, that they were there? I was wondering how they felt, and studied the men's faces to see the play of emotions. From a spectacular point of view, the results were disappointing. If their faces showed anything, it was that they were cursing the steepness of the road and the swiftness of the pace. Of any other emotions their faces were void. In their rough campaign clothes they suggested nothing so much as a crowd of men who had loitered on their way to work and were now hurrying to get there before the whistle blew. The frequent sight of picks and shovels over the shoulders of the men heightened this illusion. They were almost afraid of being "docked", yet determined to reach their work in season if speed could accomplish it. At the top of the hill they would be within sight of battle; their appearance there might be followed almost instantly by a deadly, destructive fire directed at them. Yet they showed neither eagerness nor dread nor anything but a sense that they were late on the scene.

In a dell below the top of the hill we caught sight of several teams of artillery horses, unhitched and browsing industriously in the long, sweet grass. A moment later we got a glimpse of Santiago, miles away to the southward.

Then we came to the crest of the hill, where Capron's field-pieces and guncrews stood awaiting the order to begin making things lively again. We were in sight of El Caney, too, twenty-four hundred yards away to the eastward. What a terrific din was going on over there—more racket than a dozen Fourth of July celebrations rolled into one! And here, just where things were beginning to be decidedly interesting, I was forced to drop out. It would have been a physical impossibility, just then, to have gone a hundred steps further. I felt as if walking through a furnace, and the cool shade that a tree threw over the grass proved altogether too seductive. Had I gone any further then a sunstroke would have been the reward. And yet, among civilians at home, I had been thought sturdy and enduring. The regulars still went on, showing what a difference their ceaseless training in peace times makes between them and ordinary civilians. At first I took very little interest in what was going on around me, and wondered if the sunstroke were pressing my temple in its hot hands. I took a gasping drink of water, and then lay down in the shade. After a while I felt as if a smoke would brace me up. I tried it, but had not breath enough to pull at the pipe. Down the road some more troops came into sight—the second battalion of the Third, hurrying along as the first had done. As they passed me, I rose and tried to follow them. It was out of the question, physically, as less than ten steps convinced me. If I ever go into the field again as a war correspondent I shall get to the front by easy stages, and not wait to hurry out with the reserves at the last hour.

From where I lay I had a splendid panoramic view of El Caney. I could see the village patches, the gardens and fields, beautifully laid out on the slope—and that was all. Over there one of the most famous infantry fights in history was going on. I was in a good position to hear the battle, but not to see it. With all the crashing of volleys, which never let up for an instant, there was absolutely nothing to see. The Spaniards were hidden in trenches and blockhouses around the town; our men lay upon the ground, behind sheltering ridges, or hidden in long grass or clumps of bush. The use of smokeless powder takes all the picturesque out of an infantry battle. Waiting until I found myself somewhat cooler, and able to breathe once more without it hurting, I shouldered my roll, lighted my pipe, and started on around the bend of the hill. The road lay downward, now, a blessed sight! Some two hundred yards below the battery was a spring. The water was muddy here, from the frequent visits that had been paid the spring that morning, but such a little thing is not to be minded, and after getting a good drink, I filled my canteen as full as possible. From there on a detachment of engineers was endeavoring to get the road in shape for the artillery to pass over it when the time came.

On a good bit further, and then the road led across the valley. A tolerably straight road, too, yet so rough that an exhausted man could not make swift progress over it. Ahead, coming toward me, was a young soldier, limping and leaning on a stick he had cut by the wayside. Every few steps he looked behind him at El Caney as if he wished himself back there. On meeting him, I found he belonged to the Eighth Infantry, and was swearing with all a soldier's warmth because one of his officers had ordered him peremptorily back.

"It's only a scratch," he grumbled. "They won't let me stay in hospital after tomorrow morning with it."

But afterward, eight or nine days later, I recognized him in Siboney, and that was the first day he had been allowed outside the hospital. He would have fought through the rest of the day, had he been permitted.

Behind me men were coming, stepping along with that low sound of "whump, whump" that marching men make on a muddy road. They were close upon me by the time I heard them, enough men to make about a company. They were out of breath and perspiring furiously.

"What regiment?" I asked.

"Fall in, if you want to," came the gruff answer from the sergeant at the head. I fell in, and tramped with them for a little way, but they were travelling altogether too fast for me.

So I was left to the rear again, and after a little while these men were out of sight ahead. I found out later they were men who had dropped out exhausted, and had been "rounded up". Wounded men coming back over the trail were pretty frequent by this time; they reported a good many more up near the firing line who were too badly hurt to move or be moved. There were a good many killed, too—hundreds of our men dead, so one of the shattered soldiers assured me. It was a fearful fight that was going on up on El Caney's slope; that much I could easily learn, but no details. The private soldier in a modern fight sees nothing, except in his own vicinity.

When I had gone a little further I saw a sight that made the hot blood jump. Some three hundred yards up the trail come two hospital men carrying a wounded comrade on the litter. Each bearer wore on his arm, in plain sight, the bright red cross of mercy. Soon after I caught sight of them I saw the rear bearer fall suddenly as if he had slipped. He let go of the litter and sank upon the ground a yard away from it, while the wounded man fell two-thirds off the litter before the front bearer let his end down. Hurrying forward to see if I could be of any assistance, I saw the man who had been carrying the rear end of the litter trying to bandage his left shoulder with the contents of one of the "first aid" packages, his comrade helping him.

"Shot?" I demanded.

"Of course," was the nonchalant answer from the man sitting by the roadside, while he who had been carrying the front poles growled savagely: "The sneaking dagoes are firing at every red cross they can spot!"

I offered to help, but when they found that I was a correspondent going out into the fight they declined my offer, saying that someone would soon be along to help them. During our talk the wounded man who had been riding on the litter had got back on it without help, and without saying a word.

I had only to wait a minute or two when I saw other hospital men coming up, and then hurried forward. It seemed at first thought rather surprising that the sharpshooter who had so foully disgraced his nation did not try to bring down the other hospital man or myself. His failure to do so can be accounted for only on the supposition that he had been seen and "potted" by one of our own soldiers. Earnestly do I hope that such was the case. It was the only instance I saw that day of a non-combatant being struck, but the tales told by correspondents and soldiers from all parts of the field that day are enough to make me forever skeptical when the subject of "Spanish honor" is mentioned. The soldiers of an honorable nation do not fire on wounded men and hospital attendants, as was done in scores of cases on the First of July. Later on, further at the rear, I saw plenty of wounded men being fired upon, but fortunately none that I saw was hit by this sharpshooter fire.

Meeting and passing other wounded men who were coming to the rear, I made my way gradually forward, getting nearer and nearer to the firing line. The same incessant pop-popping as of crackers was going on, but now, nearer to the scene, it sounded as if the crackers had been put under tins, for the sound was both heavier and more muffled. For the last few minutes I had heard the pretty frequent whizz of bullets. It is a startling sound at first, especially if one stops to consider the deadly capabilities of each one of these nasty pests. But one gets quickly used to it.

From time to time, when I thought the fire too hot in my vicinity, I lay down on the ground with a willingness that I am not ashamed to confess. Then, as the hoarse buzzing shifted, I would get up and, crouching, get a little further forward. I was now to the south of El Caney and a very short distance ahead of me the rifles of Miles' Brigade were crackling back a vicious answer to the guns of Spain. Yet it was only occasionally that I could see any of our soldiers, so well were they hidden while firing. And nowhere so much as a puff of smoke! The Second Massachusetts, the only regiment at El Caney using black powder, had already received orders to cease firing. Both sides were using smokeless powder.

# Chapter XI
# On the Field of Battle

It was not easy to locate either friend or foe. With all the racket, with all the hail of death raging, it looked to the spectator as if battle were being carried on without human agencies. Seeing a battle? What nonsense! There was nothing to see, unless the occasional glimpse of a blue-shirted figure raising itself to fire. Some yards ahead was a tree which did not look difficult of climbing. Determined to make the effort, I hurried forward and, leaving my roll at the base of the trunk, started up. It was a hard climb for one long out of practice, but at last I got up among the branches. It was a low palm, and the climb up that smooth trunk was difficult. But once up in the top, and fairly screened by the vegetation, I felt rewarded for all the trouble. From here there was a much better view; by comparison it was excellent. There was another advantage that I was not slow to discover, and that was that I was now above the line of fire. Bullets came at times over the ground near the base of the tree, but none so high up. My position now combined all the advantages of going to war with all the safety of being at home. Before me I could make out considerably more of Miles' men. Bushes and grass were being cut all about them by bullets coming apparently from the Spanish trenches six or seven hundred yards beyond them. And now I could see the Spaniards—no, that doesn't express it accurately either, for what I did see at the trench line up the slope was a line of bobbing hats, small enough in the distance. It was impossible to see their faces. Not even their guns were visible from my perch, but the sound of their guns was in my ears all the time. Off to the northward I had frequent glimpses of Ludlow's men; to the eastward I caught sight of troops which I did not then know composed Bates' Brigade. Chaffee's men, who were up at the northeast end of the town, I could not see at all. Miles' men appeared to be firing at a trench ahead, at a blockhouse on the left, and the famous stone fort, which was slightly to their right; at the southeast end were trenches that were being obstinately defended—trenches cut through the solid rock, it was afterward discovered.

From these trenches, the blockhouse and the fort, the firing was tremendously rapid. Thirty or perhaps a few more shots per minute can be fired from a Mauser. From the racket and the loud, angry hum of the enemy's bullets, I am inclined to believe that at that time the Spaniards were firing up to the limit. "Cutting grass" is a trite expression, but no other phrase so well describes the work of the enemy. Firing too high is the fault often imputed to the Spanish soldiery, but on this day they made few such mistakes. Few of the missiles went more than knee high, where I was, and the testimony of officers and men with whom I afterward talked was to the same effect. Personally, I was very grateful to the enemy for firing so low, for my perch was as sage as Broadway, until—Szz-zz-zz-zzzeu! That disturbing sound came within four feet of me, and went past. The sound was, or seemed, louded than a Mauser, and hoarser. Was that shot meant for me, or was it merely a wild shot? After the first startled thrill, the experience seemed a comical one.

"If that fellow aimed at me," I thought, "it proves all I've ever heard about the infernally bad marksmanship of the Spanish."

At the same time I scanned all the trees near me, even those within our own lines. While I was looking, Szz-zz-zz-zz! The second ball came, apparently, from the same direction, at about the same elevation, that is to say, just below the level of my head. But it was nearer—not more than eighteen inches away.

"That rascal is doing better—from his standpoint," I thought. "I wonder if he can really hit me."

Still I lingered up the tree, still looked. It was in a spirit of neither valor nor foolhardiness that I dallied where I was, but my perch gave me such an excellent view of the field that I hated to get down. It seemed almost unreasonable for that other fellow to expect me to, and I suppose I felt a certain amount of Yankee inclination to be independent about it and do just as I pleased. But after a little interval a third shot came. Confound that fellow! He had the range almost perfectly by this time, for this ball cut away some leaves within four or five inches of my breast. My independence vanished and, with a sudden respect for that other fellow's opinion, I began to get down out of the tree. As soon as I came to the smooth part of the trunk I slid fast. Nor did I regret my speed, for the fourth bullet struck the trunk some five feet over my head. By the time I got to the ground I was quite willing to lie as close to it as possible, until I made up my mind that the sharpshooter could no longer see me, for he didn't attempt to "get" me again.

That he was a sharpshooter, and an isolated one, I am convinced, for had he been in the enemy's trenches, in the midst of comrades, he would unquestionably have called their attention to the "good thing" in that tree, and volleys, instead of single bullets, would have come my way. I don't blame the fellow, though. He was attending to what he considered his business, and attending to it well until I interfered by getting out of his reach. I was in a very good imitation of service clothes, had a cartridge belt and revolver strapped to my waist, and he undoubtedly mistook me for an officer making a reconnaissance. Wriggling a little way from the tree, I made myself as comfortable as I could in the long grass behind a bush. But here I could see nothing except at intervals, and then what I could see did not satisfy me.

It was while lying here now that I became aware of a curious possibility on the battlefield. In the hottest fire, one may become absent-minded! From lack of ability to see well, I began to think of other matters—of home, of Broadway, of a former trip to the tropics, of the poor fare we had on the transport, and of a certain restaurant in New York where the cold salads were always a delight on a hot summer's day. I had suffered much from rheumatism in the past, and the exposure of sleeping in wet grass the night before, and the hard tramping on this day, had begun to make themselves felt by a painful stiffening. Finding my position on the ground too cramped, I rose to stretch myself, and then the combined ludicrousness and danger of this form of taking comfort dawned upon me, and I laughed and got down close to the ground again. The fire came my way again. Perhaps my own absent-mindedness had caused it. As I lay there watching the grass go down as the bullets zipped it off, I could not help wondering how many tons of hay a horse rake could take up here on the morrow. In the original plans an hour and a half had been allotted to taking El Caney. It required all day.

This is seeing battle at close range, and the spectator gets an excellent idea of what modern fighting is, where the guns are of such rapid fire and so destructive that men cannot stand up to face each other, but must advance on their bellies, rising only once in a while to fire when the enemy, also seeking a better mark, exposes himself. Up on the sides of those stone trenches around the fort, after the battle was over, was lead enough that had been fired by our men to keep a poor man in comfort for a long time on the proceeds of the sale. But knowing now what it is like to be under fire, and having a pretty good idea of what a small portion of our men are doing, I decide to go back to the hill where the battery still stands, and from there watch the progress of the whole fight, for of what is happening outside of my own vicinity I am necessarily ignorant as long as I stay here.

So I pick my way back, cautiously at first, and then rising

and going ahead rapidly as soon as it seems that I am out of range of Spanish fire. And now, on my feet, I make swift progress back. I am soon at the other side of the valley and climbing the road that leads straight up to the battery. I have seen two lines of men, six hundred yards from each other, firing rapidly and with good aim, killing and crippling each other. It seems almost madness that sets thousands of men slaying each other. It seems almost unnatural, and yet I am pagan enough to feel, as I think on what I have seen over there, at the other side of the valley, that war is really an exhilarating business; that it requires and develops the best qualities of American manhood, and that it is a fine thing to show that we are capable of taking splendidly advantageous positions away from an enemy who have always expressed for our soldiers and our arms the contempt of the ignorant.

They are learning their sad mistake today, these savage little brown men, for our lines have been steadily going forward since almost after sunrise, and going forward, too, where foreign attachés, military experts in their own lands, had predicted that we could not possibly win. El Caney is already sorely harassed and would gladly give up, as we afterward learn, were it not for one dread. Their leaders have told these little brown soldiers that *los americanos* will kill all prisoners they take, and the little brown soldiers actually believe this monstrosity. Even their subordinate officers believe it and so the fight goes sternly on, for these little brown men feel that they would much rather be killed at long than short range.

# Chapter XII
# The Taking of El Caney

There are no blunders here at El Caney. If I am to offer an explanation of the reason of this fact, I can only state that General Lawton, the division officer who is in command here, is actually on the ground, noting every move with the alert eye and the cool judgment born of much experience. He is manoeuvring the American forces on that judgment of his own, and his plan of attack is based on suggestions for which he frankly says he is indebted to a highly competent subordinate, General Chaffee, to whom in recognition is given the "best place" in the fight—that is to say, the deadliest part of the field.

But here is the spring again, and I find that I have emptied my canteen during that brief trip through the valley. So I fill it again, and then, spreading *poncho* and blankets on the grass at the roadside, lunch on my two remaining hard-tack. For the sight of death and blood do not dull the appetite of the physical man, and the scant allowance of food tastes good even when I see such of the wounded men as are able to walk toil up the path and stop at the spring. Then they go on, for further up the road, back in the rear of the battery some distance, is a temporary hospital, and there is another and much larger one on the other side of the mountains at

Siboney. With hunger somewhat satisfied, another physical need asserts itself. I must take a short nap, for the fatigue, under this blazing sun, begins to assert itself. So I compose myself on my blankets, close my eyes and am asleep at once. It is not for long, however, for overhead, a little way off, the short bang of a fieldpiece rings out and sleep must be deferred.

While I kneel over to make up my roll, I hear the hail of acquaintance. It is Brandenberg, one of the Ohio correspondents, a splendid, athletic-looking youngster in his early twenties. He is coming up the road from the valley, flushed but tireless-looking, and he immediately begins to tell me how he has been out on the firing-line at El Caney, where he has been in the trenches with our men, and describes with a good deal of earnestness how he had to wriggle on his stomach for two hundred yards back from the firing-line. He asks if I have been over there, and I reply that I have been part way. That is all I tell him, for I make up my mind that when the day is over there will be plenty of stories of correspondents' experiences to be heard by whoever cares to listen to them. In this conclusion I afterwards find I am quite correct, and from wounded soldiers later on I hear warm praise of a heroic correspondent who, under the hottest fire, at repeated risk of his life, aided them back from the firing line. The name they give to that correspondent is Earl Brandenberg, and their praises of his nerve and unselfishness is unstinted. If President McKinley finds himself with a little leisure some afternoon I doubt if he could better employ it than by writing an autograph letter to Mr Brandenberg, offering him a commission in the army in case he cares to accept it. But Brandenberg, as he now stands by me while I finish tying up my roll, tells me nothing of what he has been doing for others. When the task is done, we tramp up the hill together, and get in position just behind the gunners, who are now preparing to demolish the stone fort and such other works of the enemy as are in evidence from this position.

There are many other correspondents here, and the proprietor of one New York newspaper is also on the scene. We "swap" information freely, point out the different features of the bullet-traverse landscape, and draw rough maps for each other. Now that I have been over on the other side of the valley, and have seen what our men are doing for the honor of the flag, I find it much easier to understand the moves in the battle-game that is spread out before us.

Miles' two regiments are to the south of El Caney, while much further to the west are Ludlow's three regiments, which early in the morning had been stationed across the road between El Caney and Santiago, to shut off the enemy when they attempted to retreat to the southward. When! Nothing is clearer than that the Spanish have no such notion. Will they stay on there at El Caney, day after day, keeping up such a fearful fire that no man alive can advance and drive them out? It looks like it! No man who has read history doubts that the Spanish are brave. Their only fault is that they do not know how to fight as well as the men of some other races. But here it is easy. They are so well intrenched that none but the best troops in the world can hope to drive them out, and as to marksmanship, they have only to shoot toward our lines, firing close to the ground, and they are bound to shoot murderously. And they will not take any chance at surrender. The lie told them by their generals, that we would kill all prisoners, has worked well with these desperate, ignorant fellows.

To the north of Miles' Brigade is one in which I take a great deal of interest, naturally, for it is the one with which I marched all one night and the next morning. How are they doing? "Magnificently," is the word dropped by an officer who stands near me. And up to the northward, at the extreme right of line, Chaffee's Brigade is relentlessly closing in, though back of the brigade are rows and rows of killed and shattered men. El Caney is hemmed in—part of it taken.

Chaffee is one of the leading spirits in the rattling fight that is spread before our eyes. He it was who, days ago, has reconnoitred this field, gliding through the grass and bushes until he could hear the Spanish soldiers talking on post. He has drawn splendid maps of this field, and it is his plan of attack which General Lawton, in command of the division, has accepted, and for which he afterward gives General Chaffee full and generous credit.

There are ten American regiments in this fight, or were earlier in the day, for the Second Massachusetts, the only volunteer regiment at Caney, has been ordered to lie motionless in the grass. It is not that their courage is at fault, nor their skill. Army officers have said ungrudgingly that this splendid Bay State organization is in every essential equal to any regular regiment in the line. But the Massachusetts men are lying in the grass, doing nothing except being hit, because they are among the victims of that monumental folly of arming volunteers with old-fashioned guns that fire black powder. When the Massachusetts men fired earlier in the day each volley sent up a cloud of white smoke that hung some five feet from the ground and made their position so conspicuous that within five minutes nine men were killed and more than sixty wounded. Their low-hanging smoke not only exposed themselves but the regulars near them, and this is why, at this critical time of day, eight or nine hundred as good men as went out of America are lying useless in the grass. It was governmental murder to give these men antiquated arms and send them out against men provided with the best rifle in Europe!

Now we are treated to a splendid spectacle of what our light artillery can do at its best.

"They are getting ready to charge the fort," announces the officer. "Fire as fast as you can, and demoralize the enemy before the charge starts!"

There are four three.2-inch guns in Capron's Battery. As soon as the order is given and the range started, No. 1 gun discharges. There is a great cloud of smoke at the muzzle, and we who are standing just behind the piece see nothing but that, for the shell has struck seconds before the smoke clears. But those who stand more to one side, peering eagerly through field glasses, announce that the fort was struck.

We are happy. Doubtless a few Spaniards were killed by the fragments of shell, but what of that? We didn't come here to give the Spaniards a pleasure outing! Man is merciless when a battle is going on—merciless, but just or fiendish according to his natural temperament. Our soldiers are not intentionally firing on the Spanish wounded who are hobbling to places of comparative safety. If we are glad the shells are doing deadly work, it is more than natural. We have come on this day to feel a loathing for the Spaniard, and the more loss he suffers in ways honorable to us the better we shall be pleased. Two, three, four! Each of the guns has been fired now and every one of the shells has struck where it was aimed. Hardly has the smoke begun to lift from No. 4 gun when No. 1 is at it again, and so on down the line.

There is a whirr, not very loud nor very near, but it makes an officer turn around and ask: "Was that shrapnel?"

"No, sir," comes the reply; "that was a rifle volley."

In a few moments there is another whirr, just like the former one. It pleases us, for this effort to reach us with Mauser volleys at long range shows us how galling our shellfire has become to the sorely pressed enemy. The artillerymen are working like beavers, and the sharp, metallic sound of discharge is ringing incessantly in our ears. We laymen, who have nothing to do with the glorious work that is going on, have found positions on either flank of the battery, where, with field glasses, we can make out puffs of smoke which result from the landing of shells on the stone fort. In a few moments there is a shout of: "There are charging—splendid fellows!"

And now the firing, which has seemed to last but a few minutes, stops so far as the battery is concerned. Every shell has hit the fort, and how many do you think have been fired? I have not counted, but a man standing near me who has a taste for statistics has kept tally, and he exclaims: "Twenty-seven!"

Every field glass is being used now and we feel a strange, proud thrill. The Twenty-Fifth Infantry, negro troops with West Point officers, has just started up that hill in the face of the rain of death. What a splendid sight it is! In the distance the very uniforms look black, and the figures are tiny enough, even as thrown up on the object lenses of the glass. These figures are dropping, too—dropping faster than we can witness with composure, for these men are trying to carry the

Stars and Stripes up to the fort. It is so glorious that we feel like dancing. We have read about such deeds, but this is the first time that we have seen men of flesh and blood performing them before our eyes. They are proving that Americans have not deteriorated as fighters, and these men are black, neither better nor worse fighters than their white infantrymen and cavalrymen standing nearby, in support of the battery. They are eager spectators, and they tingle with pride at sight of the splendid work the Twenty-Fifth is doing on that slope slippery with red blood. These eager spectators can stand it no longer and keep quiet. A wild cheer rises. Surely the enthusiastic sound must reach the heroes more than a mile away. But down the line comes a stern order: "Stop that cheering!"

There is a hush in an instant, but as if aware how hard it is to stand without cheering, this explanation follows the order: "Men, if you cheer, the gunners can't hear the commands."

There are other regiments charging. It keeps us busy using the glasses. Stubborn Spain is leaving El Caney a few yards at a time. It has been a hard-fought day, but the end is nearing. Not that the popping over yonder slackens any. On the contrary, it redoubles in intensity, but that is very likely because our own men are now where they are able to deliver their own volleys with more crushing effect. Is it a fancy, or do we really hear cheering from El Caney? It sounds like it. All around me men look as if they wanted to break out singing the "Star Spangled Banner", or "My Country, 'Tis of Thee". Undoubtedly they would do it, were they not afraid of being laughed at for showing so much emotion over the whipping of so insignificant an enemy. But it must be remembered that, earlier in the day, men competent to express the opinion have predicted that we cannot whip the enemy at all. Yet now he is leaving El Caney, going backward, and firing as he goes, and the foreign experts and foreign military text-books are all wrong!

And now an order comes for the battery to hurry over through the valley, in order, if possible, to get there in time to facilitate the departure of the enemy by a few well-planted shells at close range. Horses are hitched on, men leap into saddle, the cavalry rides out into the road in single file, the artillery following, the last of all the infantry support bringing up the rear. The battle is all but over and now that the excitement is gone—merged into the certainty that Caney is ours—one scribe finds his attention called back to himself. All through the day my rheumatism has been steadily making itself more and more felt. The fatigue has not lessened the pain which temporary excitement has somewhat deadened, and two or three showers through the afternoon have reduced me to such condition that now, when I find myself gazing longingly after the departing battery, I become conscious that I had better lose no time in getting back to shelter.

There are no tents out here in the field. Mine is back at Siboney, folded up in one corner of the shack. If I stay here at the front, and sleep out again in the wet grass, morning will certainly find me utterly helpless from rheumatism. And so, though longing dictates the other way, I am compelled to decide in favour of tramping back over the mountains to dry shelter in Sibony while I am still somewhat able.

I remain on the hill only long enough to make sure that El Caney is ours beyond any possibility of a doubt, and then turn my face to the rear. From the standpoint of a chronicler it proves to be a fortunate choice, after all, for I have not gone far when I meet further proofs of the worthlessness of that thing called "Spanish honor," and I find myself in the thick of our own wounded.

# Chapter XIII
# The Trail of the Wounded

It is at the rear that an all-revealing glimpse of the horrors of the big day's fight is to be found.

On the firing line one sees men killed, or sees them wounded, or hears, perhaps, their anguished groans. Still he does not realize the horror of it all. The incessant pop-pop-popping of infantry fire is all around him, and this martial racket tends to shut out or supersede the notes of human agony. Besides, it is only here and there along the fighting line that a man is found so badly hurt that he cannot keep back groans and screams. For the most part wounded soldiers lie silent, unless it be that they are coolly chatting with prostrate comrades in the same plight as themselves. Those who are able to walk, or even to hobble, often those who are able only to crawl, make their way to the rear, in search of water first, and medical attendance afterwards. Meanwhile, those who are still with the firing line are going forward a few yards at a time and so gradually the injured men are left further to the rear, and the echoes of the agony of the worst wounded are lost to hearing. But at the rear? Now we begin to see something of the accumulated casualties of the day's work. The dead we do not see. They are lying in the roadway, at the roadside, in a tangled clump of chapparal, at the crest of a ridge, or in one of the outer trenches of the enemy's captured line of defences. When night comes, the dead will be buried with haste, close to where they fell. It will be fortunate if the dead man's chaplain is on hand to write the hero's name on a slip of paper, fold it in a bottle and drop the bottle in the grave as a means of future identification. The wounded, however, are here at the rear, making for the nearest hospital, either rapidly or slowly. The man who has a wound in the shoulder, hand, or trifling flesh wound in the side, moves along briskly. He who has received a flesh wound in the leg does not make as good progress, for the limb slowly stiffens as he goes forward. The man shot in the hip cannot walk. If he tries to crawl back, he will soon give it up. The man shot in a lung or the intestines must lie patiently where he falls until succored. Very often he dies before that succor comes.

All these kinds of wounds I see as I turn my back on El Caney and make my way slowly and painfully back along the road over which the forced march of the morning has been made. Over at El Caney the enemy have been driven out of the town, but the few hundreds who have been neither killed nor captured have retreated to the hills south and west of the town and, by pouring frequent volleys into their lately abandoned stronghold, they are doing their best to render life hazardous for the victorious Yankees.

To the southward, though Spain's soldiers have been driven back at San Juan they are, as at El Caney, firing into their victors at long range. And so the din of battle is as loud as during the more earnest fighting earlier in the day. But it is infinitely less deadly, for now our troops, too, are in blockhouses and trenches.

Not many yards have I limped along before I hear rapid steps behind me. A party of five soldiers comes along, walking briskly. Each has his left arm bandaged, with blood showing on the outer layer of the cloth, the wounds ranging in location from just above the elbow to the shoulder. One man has three wounds on the same arm. Back of the firing line, often only a hundred or two hundred yards back, surgeons and hospital men have stood or knelt in little groups, giving first care to all wounded who came their way. This first care is extremely rudimentary, from the necessities of the case, consisting only of an attempt to stop the flow of blood, and the application of an antiseptic bandage. This done, the soldier must make his own way back to where more extensive treatment is to be had. It seems curious, at first, that all of this quintette should be wounded in the same part of the body, but there is really nothing strange about it. Our troops, during the greater part of the day, have been lying on the ground or behind shallow trenches. When they fired, they exposed only the top of their heads and the left arm along which the rifle rested. Most of those who have been struck in the head are not coming back. The quintette of wounded men slow up, in order to answer questions, but they laughingly parry sympathetic remarks.

"We got off easy," they protest, "we'll be back with the regiment in a couple of days." Then faces grow a trifle grave as one of them adds simply: "You ought to see some of our boys!"

"I guess I have," is my answer. Then one of them spies a tobacco pouch hanging at my belt, and hints that a pipeful would be appreciated. In a twinkling all five are busy supplying themselves in turn. Then they are off again at the same swinging gait, for they are anxious to reach the hospital at Siboney, where they have been told that there is plenty of food and tobacco, and gentle women nurses in the garb of the Red Cross. There can be no doubt that these men are as anxious for a glimpse at pure, refreshing womanhood as they are for a sight of food and tobacco. Sick and wounded men, even of the stern soldier stuff, become children again in their wistful longing for feminine coddling and sympathy. Even in the face of so redoubtable an opposing authority as the Surgeon General of the United States army I dare affirm that one Red Cross nurse is worth two male nurses in an army hospital.

Another hundred yards to the rear and I am overtaken by three more men, all wounded in the left arm or shoulder. They, too, are eager for tobacco, for they have been days with the advance of the army, and have been reduced to smoking dried leaves, though there is plenty of tobacco in the commissary at Siboney.

And I am now frequently passed by little squads of wounded, all of them walking more briskly than I am able to do. Some have really serious wounds, but have escaped injury to the legs and so are able to walk. All who can get over the road in this fashion make light of their injuries. In many cases, however, these poor fellows are using up vital energy and death claims them a day, two days, or perhaps weeks later. Yet so far there are no fearfully wounded men on this road. We are coming to that, though. Down at the foot of this long gradual slope of road is a shallow creek that must be forded, and on the further side of the water is a little group of men.

One of them sits on the bank, with his back propped against a tree trunk. He tries to look unconcerned, but he is not talking; his teeth are too tightly clenched. He has been shot through the hip, and has been since the forenoon getting back a little more than two miles from the firing line. He stumbled through the ford, leaning on two other wounded men who had but just then fallen in with him. And now, for the last twenty minutes these two lesser unfortunates have been fashioning a crutch. It is a stout young sapling, cut to the right length, with a crotch at the top which these two men are padding for their comrade. With the aid of this crutch and such help as the two less wounded men can give him, the shattered infantryman is facing a two-mile tramp up and down along the fearful path to the nearest field hospital.

"Why didn't you wait and get a ride on a stretcher?" I ask.

"Didn't see many stretchers, and there's a heap of men hurt worse than I am," is the response. It is true that stretchers and stretcher-bearers are pitifully few, and if those who need carrying worse than this poor unfortunate fail to get it, God help them! So far I have not seen a single ambulance on the road. It makes me angry when I think of the eighty odd vehicles of best pattern that I saw on the flat cars at Tampa. In silent sympathy I hold out my tobacco pouch to the man who is waiting for his crutch. He thankfully declines; he doesn't feel like smoking, but his two comrades do, and suspend operations a moment to fill and light pipes that have been strangers to the weed for some days.

I am never out of sight of the procession of the wounded now. Some of it overtakes and passes me; other sections of it I overhaul. There are men in this long, thin straggling line of misery who are able to cover three miles an hour; others who do well if they progress a quarter of a mile in the same time. There are some who have gone as far as they can. One of these I find lying on the ground by the side of the road. He is an infantry officer, as the broad white stripe down the side of his trousers indicates, though his blouse is missing. A ball has passed clean through the bone of one leg and he has done wonders to get as far as this. Now he cheerfully assures me that he can get no farther without help. When I offer my arm, he smiles and replies that he reckons he will have to wait for his carriage. He is well supplied with water; one of the wounded men of his own company saw to that and has gone on to leave word at the field hospital where he is. He had no food and doesn't crave it. Tobacco? He doesn't care to smoke just now, but if I will be kind enough to wrap up a little in a piece of paper and put it in his pocket?

Now there are other badly wounded men who have got this far, but can get no farther. One is to be found every hundred yards or so, for quite a stretch of road, probably eight or ten of them in all. Yet everyone seems cheerful, and most of them have water, poured into their canteens by some passing comrade. Food they have not; neither have I; no one has out here at the front. My tobacco pouch grows lighter as I proceed. Still the procession of men who have been wounded, but not in the legs, goes on by me. I never overtake them again on the road, unless I find them sitting beside a fallen soldier, playing the role of ministering angel. The tender care which one wounded man gives another is something to bring tears to the eyes.

There are abundant noble samples of this Samaritanism along the road. One boyish-looking soldier has been shot through the shin-bone. It hurt a bit when he started to the rear, but he didn't mind that, and got along pretty well, until he came to the ford. Tramping through the water must have stiffened the wound, for after a while he found he could get no further. Then Lem came along, with a Mauser hole in his side, and insisted on staying with him.

And here Lem begins to talk:

"You see, he and I were brought up together. We went to the same school when we were kids. Five years ago I went into the army, and Bill, he enlisted in the same regiment in May. He just came into the service for the war, poor old chap, and I reckon he's got all he's going to get of it. I'm not hurt much—only a plug here in the side."

"I'm all right from the knee up," put in Bill, earnestly. "There ain't any sense in Lem's staying here with me, except that he's stubborn about it."

"He don't know as much about this outfit as I do," said

Lem, in an aside to me, "he doesn't know that there's mighty few stretchers and next to no ambulances with this army. The poor chap is likely not to get moved until tomorrow, or the day after, and what's he to do for water or grub, without someone to hustle for him?"

Yet even as the sight of slightly wounded, and afterwards of those who had fallen by the wayside becomes a story so oft repeated as to lose its novelty, so do such instances of splendid sacrifice for another's sake. Private Blank, of the United States army, may be uncouth or cultured, rough or gentle, but there is a true, noble, god-like heart beating under his blouse. He doesn't know how to leave a comrade in the lurch. Every now and then a man passing me by concludes from my limp that I have been hit in the leg, and promptly enquires if I need any help. Later on it makes me think unchristian thoughts when I note how slight provision has been made for these splendid fellows in hospital.

An ambulance? I haven't seen one throughout the whole day. Stretchers and bearers? There were some over back of the firing line, but none go along this bit of road to the rear. It begins to look as if a responsible somebody had imagined that this campaign was to be merely a march of triumph, instead of a theatre of carnage.

Sz-zz-zz-zz-zz-zz! That is an old, familiar sound that goes by through the trees. The singing of a bullet fails to interest me. I have heard so many earlier in the day that the sound is trite. A spent bullet—that is all.

It is wonderful how far these modern repeating rifles carry.

Sz-zz-zz-zz-zz-zz! Well, here's another! The Spaniard must be doing some pretty wild shooting. Not having any too many war relics, and knowing that I will want some, I sharpen a stick and dig down along the line of the hole. In that way, I find what went into the ground—a brass-jacketed bullet of about 45 calibre—the kind with which many Spanish volunteers are provided.

Behind comes a sound of ringing hoofs, and a mounted officer gallops along. Soon he overtakes me, and reins up long enough to say:

"If you want to get out of these woods alive, make better speed."

"Can't. Joints too stiff from rheumatism."

"Oh well, just saunter along then, if you don't care for your life.

"What's the matter?"

"These woods to your right are full of Spanish sharpshooters. They are firing on everybody who goes along this road."

With that he sets spurs to his horse and goes off at a gallop. He has already risked himself sufficiently by reining up to inform me of the danger that every man runs who loiters along this road. For this is "Sharpshooters' Lane!" This is the only road leading from El Caney to Siboney. A little further along the trail from San Juan joins it. And all through this stretch of forest, covering both roads along which must come the wounded from our day's engagements, are posted Spanish sharpshooters, some concealed in clumps of jungle, others in the thick foliage of the tops of palm trees. Armed with rifles which make but a tiny crack of noise and give forth no smoke on discharge, these Spaniards are firing on every wounded man who passes in sight. Spanish honor? What a hollow, mocking phrase!

One or two isolated cases of firing upon our wounded would not furnish an indictment against the enemy. But this is the systematically attempted murder of non-combatants who, by all the rules of war, are entitled to safety and consideration. A man wounded on the firing line throws down his gun and goes to the rear. He is no longer a soldier, an enemy. Wounded and without arms, he should be sure of humane treatment and succor, even if he should happen to stray into the enemy's camp. He cannot be knowingly fired on—so runs the law of civilized warfare. It is a law founded on chivalry and humanity, a law maliciously defied by our Spanish enemy at Santiago.

Just ahead down the road hangs a bunting that fills most men with reverence—a cross—red—the color of blood—on a background of the white of mercy and peace. It hangs in front of a big tent, the first field hospital on the march to the rear. There are straggling processions going toward it—one coming from El Caney, the other from San Juan. They meet at the door of the tent. There are ten times more applicants than the few surgeons can attend. As many as possible of the most severely wounded are taken in here; the rest are ordered to go on to Siboney where, in the great white city of hospital tents, there must be room and attendance for all who come. As I near the place, one of the surgeons comes to the door of the tent for an instant. His apron is covered with the blood of operations. He looks utterly fagged from the strain. Inside I get a glimpse of other doctors and a few men of the hospital corps. The earthy floor of the tent is sodden with blood. Only men whose lives have been all but shot out are being treated in there, each in his turn. The tent is small. It cannot accommodate "in-patients". True, there are two or three lying in there, but most of the treated are carried outside and placed upon the ground after the operation. Those who emerge from the tent, lying on a stretcher or leaning on a hospital steward are fortunate if they are not fired on by concealed Spanish sharpshooters.

At the side of the road opposite the entrance I pause, take off my roll and lift the canteen for a swallow of water. This done, I intend to speak to one of the surgeons, and tell him about the many helpless ones back on the road who have urgent need of conveyance to a place of shelter and care. But even while the canteen is being raised a soldier approaches. He is a sentry though unarmed.

"I beg your pardon, sir, but you can't stop here. You'll have to move down the road a good bit before you stop."

"Do you mind telling me why?"

"The Red Cross is flying here, and none but non-combatants are allowed to remain near here."

"I'm a non-combatant, though I wish I wasn't," is my reply.

But he points to the revolver in the holster at my belt and

tells me that unless I throw that away I must be considered a combatant. Throw it away? Certainly not, until I am sure that the last Spanish sharpshooter is well out of range. As I back off I tell the sentry that there are officers and men back along the road who are helpless and in urgent need of speedy conveyance. The reply is that all this is well known to the surgeons, and that they are doing everything as quickly as the limited means at hand will permit. Before I have backed out of his hearing, the sentry adds another piece of news to the effect that the enemy's sharpshooters have been firing through the hospital tent, despite the plainly displayed emblem of the Red Cross Society.

Here is a difference worth considering. While the Spaniards treat no condition of misery or badge of mercy as sacred, the Americans are sensitively determined that the letter and spirit of the Geneva Convention shall be observed, and so a correspondent who wears a revolver is told that he cannot linger near the Red Cross flag until he disarms.

# Chapter XIV
# In the Hospital Tent

It is only a little way down the road now to General Shafter's headquarters. Short as the stretch is, a scene takes place here that is full of dramatic interest. The Spanish sharpshooters have found out the location of headquarters and are firing upon it. A company of our infantry comes suddenly into sight around the bend where the road branches off. On they come, in columns of two, at a gait a little faster than the double quick. As they go by my place the men have their magazines open and are slipping in cartridges. It is, perhaps, fifty yards further on that they halt and line up facing the woods to the right. An infantryman, standing close to the end nearest me, catches sight of me, and motions to me to hurry on out of harm's reach. Then the line vanishes gradually through the trees. The jungle swallows up the company. They have gone into the thick tropical growth to stalk the Spanish sharpshooter. God grant them success! For a while I am so fascinated with the thought of this novel hunt that I do not want to stir, but wait with straining ears for the rifle reports that shall tell of the first finds of human game. The reports are slow in coming. When they do, it is possible only to guess whether the shots heard are being fired by this company or whether they are part of the general fusilade on the other side of Santiago valley.

So far, going to the rear had meant to follow a road nearly parallel with the valley of Santiago. Once around the bend, however, every step that carries a man further from El Caney takes him further from San Juan also. It is now that I find a fellow journeyer, a regular wounded in the shoulder who, having hurried as long as he can, now finds it best to slow down to my pace. We go on side by side, and soon come across a soldier sick with fever. He is in no hurry, either. So the three of us keep together. Frequently we are passed by wounded men on two sound legs. There being but the one trail, we see all who are traveling at better speed than ourselves. A good many of the wounded along here are negroes. They have had a good fight and are happy; wounds don't count. There is in America no such tireless man on his feet as the negro. These colored boys, most of them, seem fit to join in a foot-race.

"Let me take dat pistol ob yo'n, boss," calls out one of them as he goes by, "maybe I can shoot it straighter dan yo'."

No doubt he can, but he can travel faster too and will be well out of "Sharpshooters' Lane" long before we are, so the weapon remains with our trio. It is cocked and in my right hand, and I can't help feeling that I would give a good deal to send one of the five balls through the heart of one of the brown devils who have been firing upon us.

We three are out of sight of all others on the road for a few minutes, before we are overtaken—this time by a tall, trim-looking young soldier of hardly more than nineteen, who comes down the trail with the jaunty swing of an Englishman out for a ten-mile stroll before breakfast. His short carbine, which he is carrying over his shoulder, shows that he belongs to one of the dismounted cavalry troops that have been fighting all day over at San Juan.

"Don't you fellows think you'd better hustle out of here?" is his hail as he reaches us. "There are too many bullets flying out here for fellows that can't shoot back."

"We're making our best speed, if it is slow," I answer for all three.

"That so?" He soon acquaints himself with the particular kind of disability that afflicts each one of us, and tells us that he has been through the excitement all day without getting a scratch, and that now he is bound for Siboney to take a message to his captain, who is in hospital there.

"And since you fellows can't make any better speed," he continues simply, "I'll slow up and keep with you."

Though we all three protest that this is unnecessary, he retorts that we are by no means out of the sharpshooters' woods yet and that we may find a comrade with a Krag-Jorgensen carbine a most useful fellow. He thereupon took direction of things, and placing himself at the head, with the wounded man second and the fever patient third, directed me to bring up the rear, pistol in hand, and to keep a sharp watch on all sides. In single file thus we went forward.

"Heard anything from Aguadores?" called back the cavalryman.

"Not a word, except that one of the Michigan regiments was

to go down by the shore this morning and attack."

"I heard a little while ago that the Michiganders had to fall back. If that was so, the brown dagoes may send a detachment through from Aguadores to head off the wounded. We'll soon be opposite Aguadores, and we'd better talk mighty low, if we talk at all."

Now I understood plainly enough why the cavalryman had taken the lead. We would soon be out of "Sharpshooters' Lane" but from here to Siboney we could not tell what instant we might run into a Spanish ambuscade made up of a detachment or battalion from this eastern outpost of Santiago. Being the better-armed man, our young cavalryman took the advance as a matter of course. I shall never forget that young soldier stalking ahead of us erect and jaunty, with his carbine at shoulder-arms, and watching both sides of the trail. He was a young Californian who had recently enlisted for the war, but he looked as much of a veteran as any man in the ranks. When he noticed that the fever patient was carrying a heavy roll, he said:

"Give me that, Jack."

"Jack" demurred that he couldn't put such an imposition on another, but the cavalryman retorted silently by simply taking the roll. He carried it the rest of the way, and it wasn't a light load either, least, as often as every mile of the way we halted for a few minutes.

At one point we came upon half a dozen wounded soldiers. This was long past the limit of "Sharpshooters' Lane" and the possible ambush from Aguadores had not materialized. While we were exchanging fraternal greetings with this group, a rumbling, rattling noise came down the road. The noise came from an army mule wagon, and best of all it was empty. Faces took on an expectant look. Here was a chance for a ride all the way to Siboney. We lined up on both sides of the road, waited for the wagon to get almost upon us and then hailed the driver. He knew what we wanted before we spoke and shook his head.

"I'm blankety-blank sorry, boys, but it's against orders. I was told not to take a pound on my way back."

Soldiers know what orders are. The expectant look faded out of many faces. Some murmured, but that was all they could do. It was piteous that these men, shattered in their country's service, could not have even the comfort of a ride in one of their country's mule wagons. And by this time night was on and everyone's clothes was wet with the dew—a dew that was a good deal like rain.

"Do you mind telling me who gave you those orders?" I asked.

"Are you an officer?" questioned the driver.

"No; I am a correspondent, and I should like to know who gave orders that wounded soldiers should be denied a lift along this road—that is, if nothing in your orders prevents you from answering. The driver didn't answer, but after a moment's hesitation, replied, "It's too blankety-blank-dash bad, boys. You climb in, and I'll take the risk."

Thereupon they began to climb in. Such work is not easy for wounded men. The best way was to step upon the hub of a wheel, and from there over the tire into the box of the wagon. The young California cavalryman made himself magnificently useful in helping the crowd in.

"All right boys?" cried the driver.

"All right," came the contented chorus. There were yet miles of bad road to be covered to Siboney. This ride was a Godsend. It was a recompense for the painful tramp that had preceded it. Yet no sooner had the mules started than every man in the wagon changed his mind. The wagon was without springs, and the jolting was indescribable. Men who had painful wounds must have been in agony as the springless wagon jolted and jounced over the bumpy road. But they proved themselves game. An eighth of a mile further on, the driver pulled out into a clearing.

"This is as far as I go, boys," he announced. No one was sorry. All got out in the same painful way they had got in and, after thanking the driver, toiled onward. After that, had any mule wagons with accommodating drivers passed, we should have continued to walk. Gradually the rest pulled ahead. Our quartet was left by itself in the stillness and darkness of that Cuban forest. And now we began to hear a strange rustling in the woods. At times it moved across our path. It was a hideous sound, caused by the most repulsive creatures that crawl over the earth, the Cuban land crab.

In shape and characteristics of gait these land crabs resemble the kind we are accustomed to in the United States, but they are of a dirty stone color. They do not take to the water but infest the shore, the forest, and even up into high mountains. They are carrion feeders. Corpses were found in the woods afterwards with hundreds of these hideous scavengers swarming over them. In a few minutes they will pick a human being's bones clean. They are not a whit less voracious than the turkey buzzard and they are far more numerous. By night they roam everywhere in the forest, and the sound they make in crawling over the twigs and dried leaves is enough to drive a healthy man to insanity. Their scent for carrion is amazing; the faintest odor of blood is said to be sufficient to attract them from a considerable distance. It was the passage of hundreds of wounded men over the trail that night that brought these hideous things swarming by the thousands. Thousands? It may be that such a word gives too mild an estimate of the numbers. Once when I halted to light my pipe, I remember that my comrades counted some twenty crawling in the trail ahead and behind us within the small circle of light made by the burning of the match. As we tramped along we often had to use a little care to avoid stepping on these pests. Our cavalry companion did step on one, but the crunching sound and the vile odor were so sickening that all four of us took pains not to repeat the accident. Had a wounded man fallen by the roadside, unconscious that night, in this forest, he would unquestionably have been devoured. These are gruesome details to print, but they are essential to the picture of that fearful night march of the wounded. It was rustle and click-click on every side for miles as the hungry creatures roamed about in search of a fulfilment of the promise that the scent of blood carried to them.

At last we came to Guasimas, where the Rough Riders had had their first memorable fight just a week before. There, close to the roadside, was a little plot, roughly laid out, with seven low mounds. Hats came off instinctively. "Brave men," said one of our quartet softly as it was an epitaph and a prayer in two words. After going a little way the trail looked unfamiliar. Footsore, famished, drenched with dew and fagged out, we could not serenely contemplate the chance of being lost overnight in this hideous forest. But one of our number caught sight of a wire hanging overhead. It was the telephone wire put up by the signal corps, connecting General Shafter's headquarters with Siboney. Its whole length had been laid along the "Mountain Trail", as this upper path was called to distinguish it from the wagon road which branched out near Guasimas. We were on the right path, then, and followed it confidently with the overhead wire for a guide. Now what a welcome sound came to our ears! It was the beating of the strong surf against the rock-bound coast. Finally we came to the crest of a hill from which we caught sight of the moonlit bay of Siboney. The lights on the cluster of transports and gunboats there twinkled a friendly, cheering welcome. A fresh spurt carried us to Blockhouse Hill, where a large company of Cubans was encamped about the block-house. They had been valiantly defending this unattacked place all day long, while Americans, twelve or fourteen miles nearer Santiago, fought the battle that set Cuba free! We did not stop to look at them, ignored their greetings, went down the last long, steep descent and were in Siboney.

At this time, I should say from memory, there were about thirty hospital tents in Siboney. They were full. There was a long line of wounded men awaiting attention. More were coming constantly. In the meantime, soldiers and hospital men were putting up more tents. At the operating tables regular and contract surgeons were as busy as men could be. Hospital stewards and men were rushed, but rushed apparently under good system. The five Red Cross nurses spent most of their time around the operating tables. It was evident that they were considered of the greatest value. It is dismaying to think what would have happened to our poor shattered boys at Siboney if the Red Cross women had remained behind in the United States. How much more might have been done had the numbers of Red Cross women in Cuba at that time been twenty-five instead of five.

All night long the wounded tramped in, took their place in line and waited. Saturday morning they were still coming. That morning I found myself somewhat recovered from the rigors of the day before, but still in no condition to go to the front. I went to the hospitals, instead. Before leaving Tampa, I was fortunate enough to think that there might be many men in hospitals who would want letters written, and had provided myself with an abundance of paper and envelopes. I took a good supply of these with me when I went to the hospital. To make the rounds took me the entire day. Going to the head of each tent, I asked who wanted letters written home. Scores of soldiers, lying bandaged on their blankets, accepted the offer.

Others thanked me and said they would be satisfied with an envelope or two and a few sheets of paper, and would write for themselves. Most of those who used me as their amanuensis were men too badly shattered to be capable of writing. Yet nearly all of these dictated letters which told their dear ones at home that they had received but trifling injuries. Stern moralists have declared that there are no such things as white lies, but I must disagree with them. The letters in which soldiers told anxious ones at home that their wounds were but trifling struck me at the time as being lies well nigh holy. And once reasonably sure that his folks at home would not have cause to worry much over his condition, the badly wounded soldier settled down on his blanket with an easier mind as an aid towards his ultimate recovery.

Friday night the doctors did not sleep. Saturday was one of incessant work. Many of the surgeons performed or assisted at more operations on Saturday than had fallen to their lot in all their years of previous practice.

Out at the front, on this Saturday, more were being wounded. Lawton's division, victorious at El Caney, had moved southward to reinforce Kent and Wheeler, and the relentless American line was drawn close around the city. Bates' brigade had performed wonders in the way of marching, Thursday night spent on the road, Friday in marching and then fighting at EL Caney. After dark came the burial of the dead. Then, at about 10 pm, they marched to San Juan by a devious course, reaching their new position after 2 am. At daylight on Saturday, the battle began again for them, as for all the other American troops. Saturday night the Spaniards, who had seen the Americans charge hills and take intrenchments under withering fire, tried it for themselves. That laughable fiasco, the night sortie of the Spaniards, again showed their commanders that there is a great difference between American and Spanish troops.

Saturday's work, while not as bloody as Friday's had been, still contributed scores more of wounded men to the great field hospital at Siboney. Here under tents, washed, probed and bandaged, our boys in blue were asking a new and serious question: "When do we get something that we can eat?"

Army rations there were, such as hearty healthy men can eat, but there was a ghastly lack of food suitable for the sick and wounded.

# Chapter XV
# The Hospital Service

"I'm brain-fagged and body-tired," declared the doctor, halting in front of the porch and resting both elbows on the bench that ran the whole length of the outer edge of the porch.

He had come down through Newspaper Bay, as we had dubbed that part of the main street of Siboney. Here were three buildings which had been seized and occupied by war correspondents. It was the principal gathering place of the little Cuban town. Here the correspondents came when they returned from the front; here they wrote their despatches and the longer stories that went by mail; here obliging officers came who had some new item of news. Foreign attachés dropped in too to hear what news had escaped them, and in return they were sometimes lured into expressing more or less trenchant opinions of how the campaign was being conducted. Here, too, the home-going mail had been received and cared for. Hence Newspaper Row became an exchange—a sort of forum. Everyone who wanted to hear or tell something came our way.

It was Sunday morning, July 3rd, a beautiful, clear day, an ideal American day, one of the passing officers explained, with no notion of how prophetic his words were. While the heat was all that is conveyed by the word "tropical", yet it was tempered by the breeze blowing in from the sea that was but a few yards from our porch, and he who could sit back in the shade found nothing to grumble at in the weather.

"They're still coming—poor fellows," sighed the doctor, taking a few tired whiffs at the cigarette which had been offered him. "They're coming a good deal faster than we can attend to them, though we are going without sleep in the effort to catch up with our work. Few of us have had forty winks since Friday, though several naval surgeons have come ashore and are helping us splendidly."

Out at the front the fighting was still going on. Friday's was the big battle, but Saturday had seen some sad work in a lesser degree, and a correspondent who had just got in from the front informed us that at daylight on this Sunday morning our forces had again gone at the work of hammering Santiago. Having pretty completely invested the city, all that was now left for the Americans to do was to take it by assault.

"I am told that means from three to five thousand more men will be killed and wounded on our side," mused the doctor aloud. We had heard the same estimate and believed it. And, once our army got into the city, Cervera was there in the harbor, to pound the victors with his great guns. A city which could be captured only by the grandest heroism and at frightful loss would probably prove untenable to the victors, who would have no artillery capable of effectively replying to Cervera's fire. Victory and destruction looked like twin terms.

Even now our hospital at Siboney was overcrowded, the

whole force of doctors, stewards and nurses overworked to the point of collapse. The assault and capture of the city itself, and then in turn the bombardment of the victors—no wonder the surgeons were in a condition of wondering dread! The sacrifices to victory seemed destined to become one of the most harrowing pages in the annals of war. Every few minutes some of the wounded arrived from the front.

No man who could use his feet was allowed to ride. All of the transportation by vehicle was reserved for the wounded who could not possibly walk. How many ambulances does the reader imagine there were with us in Cuba? Three! And they were there by the merest luck. Bates' Brigade had sailed from Mobile with the three ambulances belonging to that organization. The eighty odd sent to Tampa by rail did not come to Cuba with us. Lack of transportation facilities was one of the excuses urged. Yet in time of war the United States Government has authority to seize any vessel needed for transport purposes—making proper payment later on, of course.

Now, even refusing carriage to any man barely able to use his legs in getting back to Siboney, it is quite apparent that three ambulances could not bring in all the wounded men who could not walk. The round trip out to the front and back was twenty-eight or thirty miles, and over a road or path which made even one round trip a day a remarkable performance. So mule wagons were called into service. These tough, durable vehicles are intentionally constructed in a way that makes it possible to haul them over fallen trees, small boulders, through mud two feet deep, and in general over and through any kind of a road that is wide enough for the wheels to pass. These wagons are springless. A healthy man, troubled only with aching feet, would sooner tramp fifteen miles than try to ride the distance in an army mule wagon. And these were the vehicles which, in the absence of a proper number of ambulances, were made to serve in their place. In the cases of very seriously wounded soldiers it was necessary to get them to the hospital somehow; it would be interesting to know how many men died from the jolting they got.

The foregoing can give but a faint idea of the horror of the situation on Sunday morning, when it was believed that it would be necessary to take Santiago by assault; when it was thought that the main battle of the campaign was still before us, with all the frightful losses it must entail. It made the heart sick and the brain dizzy to contemplate the prospect when already the facilities of the surgical department were so woefully overtaxed. Yet the heads of the medical department of the army in Washington have since asserted that every contingency conceivable to human foresight had been amply provided for! Go tell that to the men who were in Siboney at that time! Go tell that, too, to the foreign military and naval attachés who saw the situation and contrasted it with the system in the medical departments of the armies which they represented! The sad truth is that in a campaign where men died in droves, both by bullet and by tropical disease, the medical and surgical provisions were not ample, nor even tolerably ample.

The mule wagons that passed our shack that morning, each carrying eight or ten gallant fellows shattered in the service of their flag, were surely not a part of that "ample provision". It would have been an act of inhumanity to make the enemy's wounded who fell into our hands ride in such conveyances. As far as might be, comrades of the wounded men who rode in these mule wagons had tried to make them comfortable for the trip. Clothing, leaves, grass—anything soft—had been placed in the bottom of some of these substitute ambulances, to relieve some of the fearful wear and tear and rack of the journey. There were no covers over them. Helpless—sometimes unconscious—they were obliged to ride fifteen miles with the tropical sun blazing on their faces. Some of the comrades out at the front had tried to keep sun rays out of the sufferers' faces by rigging up palm and other leaves over them.

In the meantime, troops out at the front were suffering pangs of hunger. The quartermaster's department had been blamed for the failure to get food to them. There could have been wagon-loads more of it sent there, had it not been that so many of the quartermaster's vehicles were diverted to the more imperative work of bringing in the wounded. In this way the lack of adequate provision of ambulances by the medical department greatly hindered the quartermasters in the transportation of food to the fighting part of the army. Logically, the surgical department not only caused the wounded unnecessary and untold agony, but also caused other thousands, still passably well, to weaken and sicken through the lack of sufficient food.

Along towards ten o'clock I went up to the hospital again with paper, pencil and envelope, for there were always scores of men who wanted letters sent home. The wounded were lying on the ground, generally on a single blanket spread over the hard-caked earth. Cots? Well, there were a few. So close were the men lying to each other that I had to exercise the greatest of care in getting through. Here and there, when I wrote a letter for a soldier, it was possible to kneel on the ground between two men; but in rather more cases it was necessary to stand up—and to stand in the smallest possible space. The Red Cross nurses, being more experienced and less clumsy, managed the problem better. The amount of work those five heroic women could do in an hour was a marvel.

"How do you like the Red Cross sisters?" I asked one of the men.

"They're the only good thing here," was the gulping answer.

Another, for whom I was writing a letter home, paused after dictating a few short sentences, then added:

"Tell mother the Red Cross nurses are a little below the angels!"

The hunger which had begun on Saturday was intensified by now. On every hand there was complaint of lack of food. Soldiers who said they were hungry held up hard-tack nibbled around the edges, or showed me cans of baked beans.

"Fine stuff for men in pain and with blood afire, isn't it?" asked one of these food exhibitors.

"If I could have a little gruel—" said one, wistfully.

"Or a glass of milk," suggested another.

"I'd like an orange—it would be a square meal and a good drink afterwards for me, today."

"I kain't eat dem beans. Done tried to, but dey turns mah stummack," complained a negro trooper. "Ef I could hab one good slice ob watermelon—"

This raised a laugh. It took but little to amuse the good fellows.

One regular in that tent had been shot in more than one place. He was pretty well covered with bandages. Between him and the hard ground was a single fold of blanket. If he could have had a cot to lie upon it would have been comparative comfort, but he was in great pain and the little ridges of ground under him made a bed of torture. He had tried repeatedly to shift himself into a somewhat more comfortable position; he had had the assistance of one of the hospital stewards. It was out of the question, though. There was no soft side to that ground, and no one position that was more comfortable than another. He gave it up, finally, and began to cry—not from bodily pain, but from sheer misery. As I came toward him he looked up and said, brokenly; "Pardner, will you tell me something?"

"What is it?"

"For God's sake, what kind of country have I been fighting for?"

I didn't answer that question; it was too much of a poser. Instead, I tried to tell him that things would soon be in better shape. He listened to me with marked incredulity. On a later day, when I looked for him, he was not there. He had died, wondering what kind of a country had received the sacrifice.

Just before noon we paid a visit to the camp of some hundred and sixty Spanish prisoners who had been brought in from El Caney. They were encamped in the open, up at the southwest end of the village—a dirty, sullen, but picturesque looking lot of undersized men. They were still wondering at what hour they were to be shot to death, for their officers had told that this was their certain fate should they fall into the hands of the American barbarians.

Around this camp of prisoners was posted a strong guard of Michigan Volunteers, intended not so much to hinder the escape of the Spanish as to prevent the Cubans from making an attempt to get at them with machetes. We found them well provided with rations, issued by our commissary at the rate of three good square meals a day for each prisoner. When asked if they had any complaint to make about their treatment, several of the soldiers replied at once that they had not once fared as well since leaving Spain. The two officers who belonged to this outfit had been given quarters in the blockhouse a few yards away.

Walking down the street again to "Newspaper Row" we were just in time to see a couple of mule wagons coming up the street, escorted by mounted cavalrymen, carrying rifles rampant from the right knee. That escort meant more prisoners, and we hurried forward to get a glimpse of them. There were about a dozen in the two wagons, and one of the troopers obligingly informed us that he had heard they were some of the enemy's sharpshooters who had been rounded up. Nearly everyone in the lot was wounded. There was one who was not, and he was not a Spaniard, but a foreign correspondent who had come down with us on the *Olivette*. Out at the front he had been acting queerly, as if he were trying to break through to the enemy's lines. Twice he was arrested and released; the third time he stayed arrested, on suspicion of being a spy. He pooh-poohed and claimed it was all a personal dispute with some of our officers. Had he been convicted he would have been shot. In the absence of positive evidence to warrant this fate, he was subsequently shipped out of the island.

Dinner over, news came that electrified us. It was that Cervera's fleet had made what seemed a foolhardy dash from Santiago harbor, and that all the vessels except the *Cristobal Colón* had been promptly destroyed. The Oregan was reported to be in chase of the *Colón* and gaining on her. As soon as we were in possession of the first scant details, several of us hurried up to the hospital to carry the great news to the wounded. There was no cheering because of hospital regulations, but the happiness of the men lying there shone in their faces.

Outside was the wildest excitement. The first crowd of men to hear the news let out a cheer than shook the air. So did the second. After that the cheers traveled faster than the news. Everyone in Siboney knew that some great cause for jubilation was afloat, so those most remote from Newspaper Row cheered first and came down afterwards to find out what it was about. Next the big transports out in the bay took it up, trying to drown the cheers with loud steam-whistle notes, and up on a hill to the eastward flew an American flag. One soldier, unable to show his great joy in any other way, raced to the flag-pole, seized the halliards, and fairly made beautiful Old Glory dance a jig. The noise continued full twenty minutes. Then every man settled down to talk about it with someone else, and there was thirst and hunger for more details. It was not long before these came, impersonated by Captain Paget, of the British Royal Navy. His was a figure that every American who was in Siboney will long remember. A tall, spare, well-built man of probably sixty who invariably wore a linen uniform, visored cap and monocle, and who appeared inseparable from his "stick" and long telescope. He would out-tramp any youngster of twenty, had a seeming faculty of being always in the right place at the right time to see what was going on, and an obliging habit, that endeared him to us all, of promptly coming to tell us whatever he saw that was newsy. At San Juan, when he saw our flag floating from the heights after the famous charge, he jumped up and down in his delight, shouting, "The victory is ours!"

When at El Caney he saw our brigades charge up and take positions which his fighting experience had led him to declare impossible a few hours before, he actually cried to think that he had lived to see such a day and men of such bravery as Uncle Sam's soldiers. He was at all times a sincere admirer of American fighting prowess and now, as he came in fresh from the naval battle which, with his persistent good luck, he had been on hand to see, he trembled and beamed at the same time with satisfaction.

"Er—er—by Jove—the greatest thing—er—er—that I ever—er—saw. Cervera's ships came out shooting and—er—er—er—er—er—er."

"Go on, captain," we begged breathlessly.

"Er—er—er—and it was all over, by Jove!"

But presently he added that the *Colón* was off and away, but with the *Oregon* in full chase, and ready to follow to Cape Horn or Spain, if necessary. When we inquired if the *Oregon* had a good show to catch up with the *Colón*, Captain Paget look injured.

Then he enthusiastically declared that if the Americans always fought on land and sea the way he had seen them do during the last few days, it wouldn't take an Anglo-American alliance six months to whip the allied rest of the world.

Captain Paget and one other naval attaché happened to be on one of the transports that was pretty far out at the moment when the naval fight began. The captain of that transport had persistently refused, much to the discomfiture of the two attachés, to go nearer to the fight than seven or eight miles, but even at that distance, with the aid of their powerful glasses, they had been able to follow the course of the combat in detail. When it was evident that several of the Spanish craft were sinking, Captain Paget begged the master of the transport to steam nearer in order to extend humane assistance to Spaniards floundering in the water. The master of the transport, however, refused, thinking he was already quite near enough to the fight. This cowardly refusal the Briton, it was plain to see, regarded as the only blot on the grand American performance, and he gave the master of the transport a pretty bluff hint of his opinion.

Later on we heard another detail of the fight, or rather a side scene of it, that was calculated to make magnanimous blood boil. Some of the wrecked Spanish sailors, swimming to the shore, fell into the hands of Cuban men and women, who at once proceeded to machete them.

This Captain Evans saw through his marine glasses, and the *Iowa* promptly threw a few shells into the inhuman Cubans, another act by which "Fighting Bob" has endeared himself to fairplay-loving Americans.

With the Spanish fleet out of the way it now seemed certain to us that the American assault upon Santiago would begin at er—er—er—once. It might be taking place and was likely to continue two or three days. Then correspondents began coming in rapidly from the front to write their dispatches.

In the meantime the insufficient number of attendants at the hospital had been working ceaselessly for three days. If one will consider the awful strain of day and night work on trained nurses in a hospital at home, one may gather a dim notion of the stern courage that was necessary to a nurse in the hospital service at Siboney. At home every appliance, every convenience, every aid is prompt at hand. In the camp hospital, men were sick, suffering and tarnished or wrongly fed, and every trifling requisite to the nurse's science was troublesome or difficult to secure.

It occurred to some of us that though we were untrained, we might be of some use up there under the rows of white tents. I went up to inquire of Major Lagarde whether he could use a few willing amateurs.

"I can make use of all who come," was the quick answer.

"Some of us will be here this evening, then."

A squad of volunteers was organized. Major Lagarde's orders were simple and easily comprehensible.

"Sit on that bench outside," he directed. "When you hear a shout for 'hospital man', go where the shout comes from. Go in turn, so as to divide the work. Do whatever the surgeons or stewards tell you to."

That looked easy. But before there was any call for our services, Major Lagarde himself came toward us, told us that two of the Red Cross nurses had found twenty minutes in which to make gruel for some of the sick men, and directed us to go and bring it down in cups. We hurried off up to the house where two pails of gruel were ready. The nurses had been summoned back to the operating tables and could cook no more. They were even unable to go with us to show us the patients who need the food most. We must go through and find out for ourselves. We went. The appearance of the steaming, delicious stuff created a sensation. But there was not enough to go around. Promising the still hungry ones that we would get some more somehow, we went back to the Red Cross hospital. There, in the back yard, we found a kindly old gentleman named Bangs, a sanitary engineer connected with the Red Cross. He gave his life to his country, as it afterwards proved, at Siboney.

Ritchie and I offered to do the cooking if he would show us how.

"How much time can you give to this?" asked Dr Bangs.

"Until daylight, or noon tomorrow, if necessary."

He thereupon instructed us. It was not difficult, but it was certainly slow work. There were only two small charcoal braziers. Such fires were slow, and had to be frequently and vigorously fanned. Water had to be heated to boiling, but we got it under way and kept it going. In each batch of gruel a bottle of malted milk and a can of condensed milk were emptied. There was no lack of materials. The Red Cross ship, *State of Texas*, out in the bay, had seven tons of oatmeal on board which had been brought for this purpose. All through the night we went on making the hot, savory stuff, and Bennett and Donohue, provided with buckets, cups and lanterns, went through the rows of tents offering gruel to all who wanted it.

"To make the boys feel better," laughed Bennett, "we have told them that the nurses are making this gruel. One soldier swallowed his with a good deal of relish, lay back on his blanket contented, and said that it beat all Hades how these Red Cross girls could make old-fashioned gruel."

The wounded men who had been unfed for three days could not realize that there was now promise of an unlimited supply. In consequence, many a hungry fellow would look up wistfully when the food was offered him—then indicate someone else in the tent who needed it more. On one of the rounds, when I went through, a young officer replied that he'd certainly be mighty glad of a cupful. Then, as I got nearer he raised himself on one arm, peered into the bucket and added: "You haven't much there. I guess you can skip me, but there's one of my men over there whom I wish you'd give a cupful to."

Both men got all they could swallow. Thus the "gruel-squad" came into being. It went on duty every evening as long as the need continued, other correspondents and some of the soldiers taking turns. Every pound of material for this work came from the Red Cross people.

The Fourth of July was the strangest one which most of us who were there ever saw, or are likely to see. There was no fighting going on at the front. The truce was likely to last indefinitely. Siboney was a place evenly divided between work and sorrow and suffering. There was no time for jubilation. It was on this day, if I remember rightly, that we found Captain Stevens of the Signal Corps. His face was flushed with fever. He had eaten nothing for four days.

"I came here," he explained, "because I thought my men might be able to find time enough to attend to me. It was a mistake. They didn't have a moment to spare, they are driven so by work that must be done."

Then he told us about the four days without food. Two of us started off to get it. Where? At the Red Cross hospital, of course, where such things were kept. Soon the captain had swallowed a cup of hot malted milk. By his couch were left some soda crackers and a jar of jelly—little things, but all he wanted.

Up at the camp of Spanish prisoners a different kind of hardship existed, or at least was alleged to exist. The two Spanish officers who lived, as already stated, in the blockhouse, were visited by an American correspondent. They complained, indignantly, that they were not allowed any opportunity to bathe. The correspondent repeated this to the officer of the guard, a Michigan officer.

"They can't get baths, eh?" repeated the lieutenant, his eyes twinkling. "I'll have that remedied at once."

Two minutes later there was a knock on the door of the blockhouse. When one of the Spanish officers opened the door, he found himself confronted by an American officer and a squad of men.

"We have come to take you to your bath," said the American, politely. This announcement, in connection with a squad of armed men, looked rather peculiar. The Don made some reply about not caring for a bath, just then. He might as well have saved his breath. The American officer was courteous, but firm. His orders were that the prisoners were to bathe. Before the Spaniards got through objecting, they found themselves marching in the center of a squad of men headed for the beach. They reached the edge of the bay at a point where there were no other bathers.

"There is your bath ready for you," said the American officer, pointing to the ocean. Again the prisoners demurred, but were informed that a bath had been ordered, and could not therefore be avoided. Being officers themselves, they must know the inviolability of orders. Surely, as gentlemen, they would not force the American officer to the highly regrettable necessity of—of—"

Slowly, but surely, it dawned upon the nettled Dons that this bat was an affair that could neither be dodged nor postponed. They objected to being asked to disrobe before these soldiers, but the American officer pointed to a distant part of the beach where American officers and men were bathing together. Unfortunately their status as prisoners precluded the courtesy of sending the guard back. So with some anxiety they stripped, then they looked at the water, next back at the line of guards, and then, acting upon a gentle hint, went into the water. There they stood, half up to their knees, until it was made plain to them that the guards were there to see to it that they had as thorough a bath as the facilities permitted. When the American officer left them at the door of their blockhouse quarters later, he added: "I am permitted to promise you that you shall have a bath once a day hereafter. Should you desire two per day, I think it can be easily arranged."

No fault can be found with our treatment of the Spaniards. Even the refugees who came out of Santiago subsisted on army rations, provided with a free hand. A captain who went out to El Caney with a provision train intended for the use of the Spaniards, was confronted by Cubans with arms in their hands, loudly declaring that they had much more claim upon the rations than any Spaniard could have. When the American officer curtly declined to be held up in this fashion, the Cubans started to make a rush on the train. In a twinkling the officer sprang from his horse and drew a pistol. The captain snatched it from his hands, and then shouted firmly, "If you fellows try any more nonsense, I'll order my men to fire into you!"

Slowly and sullenly, with a good deal of declamation, our so-called allies withdrew. They could have had plenty of provision by sending a number of packers back to Siboney. But this they were too lazy or too lordly to do. Much as our soldiers detested the Spaniards, they rather preferred them to the Cubans.

One evening, just after dark, Lieutenant Hobson, of *Merrimac* fame, rode in, accompanied by Colonel Astor. Mr Hobson got a rousing reception in an instant. Army officers crowded forward to clasp the naval hero's hand, saying, "I am lieutenant so-and-so," or "Captain this-and-that." The hand-shaking was terrific. A dense crowd of soldiers stood around, looking on wistfully. Finally one of the privates stepped forward with, "I'm Private Dash, of the Thirty-Third Michigan, but I'd like to shake hands with you, Mr Hobson." He did, and after that scores more of the enlisted men had their chance. Then the Lieutenant sat patiently in saddle, answering all of our questions, for the next half hour, as to how he had been treated in Santiago. He left us under fire of volley after volley of cheers, and as the boat bearing him sped over the water, every warship and transport in the bay joined in the din of steam-whistles.

A half hour later we had another hero, in the person of Able Seaman Murphy of Hobson's famous dare-devil crew. His reception was no less intense than his officer's had been.

We needed things to make us cheer in those terrible days. The procession of wounded was now replaced by a longer procession of sick men, who straggled in constantly for treatment. Malaria, dysentery, mountain fever and typhoid were rife. There were suppressed whispers that yellow fever had broken out, though as yet no confirmation could be secured. Yet even those who scoffed at the actual presence of it knew that it could not be long before Yellow Jack would be stalking through the camps.

# Chapter XVI
## The Close of the Campaign

"I hear there's some yellow fever around here?"

The soldier who made the statement, half interrogatively, had come to Siboney from the front during the truce in early July.

It was said in front of our shack, and as the correspondent to whom the remark was addressed did not reply, the soldier persisted.

"It is true?"

"I asked the doctor," replied the correspondent, "and he said there wasn't a case of yellow fever in this part of Cuba."

A little more than half satisfied, the soldier went off.

The correspondent's statement was true—the doctor had denied that there was any yellow fever. It was a part of his particular business to deny it. By this time the surgeons were treating several assured cases of the yellow plague, but they were denying it under orders. Most of the men with the Fifth Army were from the northern states. They had had no experience with yellow fever, and dreaded the very name of it. They were prepared to believe that any man who got yellow fever might as well have his death certificate written at once. So, after it began in Siboney, army surgeons denied its existence as long as possible. For the same reasons, the correspondents denied it too. The first few cases were hurried off to a sequestered camp up in the hills. It was hoped in this way to limit and stamp out the plague.

What first caused the outbreak? That is a question which I believe the army's medical officers haven't ceased discussing. The most probable cause was disregard of the order of General Miles, issued before the expedition left the United States, to burn every building near which Amercian troops were encamped. Siboney had been a center of the plague in years past. There was probably not a building there which was not infected with germs of the disease. If all the houses had been burned as soon as American soldiers reached the town, it is probable that the outbreak, if it occurred at all, would have been of much less extent. At Guantánamo, where the marines did burn every house as soon as they landed, there were no cases of yellow fever.

All this time the men of the corps had not medicines enough. Medicines in plenty had been brought down from the United States. Where were they? Out on the transports. It has since been claimed that the medicines were loaded haphazard on the first convenient ships at Tampa, and that when we reached Cuba no one knew on which ships most of the medicines were. It has also been claimed that it was impossible to get transportation for these medicines from the ships to shore. Such excuses should count for very little. If there were no officer in Siboney who could be spared for the work of getting the medicines ashore, there were a good many civilians there who might have been utilized, and who would cheerfully have lent their services.

Some of the men belonging to our party of correspondents were ill. It kept the rest of us busy a good part of each day skirmishing for medicines and for such food as sick men can eat. Malaria was supposed to be their ailment. One day in the early afternoon I went up the street to the hospital to find a surgeon and I encountered Dr Guiteras, the yellow fever specialist. He had already been down to see some of our men, and I asked him to come down again that afternoon.

"Oh, I have something to say to you," replied Dr Guiteras, fumbling in his pocket and bringing out some slips of paper. "Are you ready to do something for me? Very well, then. I wish you would get Major Romeyn and Mr Ewan ready to go up to the fever hospital. See that their baggage is packed to go with them."

The fever hospital stood on the street just back of ours. It was a large wooden building where men suffering non-infectious fevers were sent to be treated.

"And at the same time," continued the doctor, "have Bennet and Steep, with all their belongings, ready to go up the country on the train when it starts this afternoon."

"Up the country? Have they got the yellow fever?"

Dr Guiteras looked at me quietly for a moment before he replied:

"Yes."

Up to that time, death had not touched the correspondents. Four had been wounded while watching the fighting.

Going back to the shack, I told the four sick men the

doctor's orders. I told Bennett and Steep that they were to be taken up into the hills, where it was considered healthier than on the coast. Maxwell and I got the baggage in readiness to be moved. After that, water was heated over a camp fire and each of the sick men had a drink of hot malted milk—obtained at the Red Cross Hospital. Seeing troops landing on the beach, I turned to go down there to see what regiment it was. Before I had gone many steps I met a man in private's uniform who asked, "Where is my sick brother?"

Only a glance was needed to show that he was the brother of Bennett.

"Come around the end of the house," I said.

There, out of sight of the sick men, I told Private Bennett what was the matter with Correspondent Bennet, adding:

"We haven't told him yet he has yellow fever. You can use your own judgment about that."

It must have been a shock to the young soldier to land on that pest-ridden island and receive such news. He was too game to show it, however.

"I'll go up and see Jimmie," he said.

For an hour the brothers talked, Private Bennett giving his brother all the latest home news and cheering him up wonderfully. Then the train, consisting of an engine and a single freight car, came and stopped opposite the shack a few yards from our porch. The brother in uniform helped the other one to the car. After watching it out of sight, Private Bennett shouldered his musket and went off to report to his captain.

An hour later this young soldier with the anxious heart was somewhere in the ranks of the First Illinois, marching over the mountain trail to the front. Fortunately all of our party who suffered from yellow fever recovered.

Back of our shack was a sad spectacle that was provided for onlookers during every hour of the daylight. As I sat by the window I would hear the sharp, metallic plink-plank. There was no need to look up. I knew what it meant. Whenever I did look, however, I saw two or three men in the uniforms of privates at work with picks and shovels, digging a shallow trench some six feet long. Lying near by on the ground would be a plain wooden box, or more often merely a figure wrapped in a blanket. When the trench was ready, a chaplain would pronounce a brief service, and then the grave would be covered up. Very often, while watching one burial from the window, I would see the small procession of two or three others.

Just outside the window stood a soldier one morning. He was watching the all too frequent spectacle of three burials at once, and there was a reflective look in his eyes.

"I reckon there's a half dozen hearts back in the United States going into every one of those holes up the hill," he observed.

There were many heroes of stern and noble material among our surgeons. The hero of Siboney was Surgeon Major Lagarde, of the regular army, in charge of the hospitals. In that trying climate he performed the work of three men for weeks. Despite his magnificent physique, it is a marvel that he lived through it. He was humane, tender and energetic. Soldiers loved him. Dr Guiteras, the Government's yellow fever expert, was another indomitable, unceasing worker. Surgeons Ireland and Lawrence followed nobly the pace set for them. Dr Parker, a civilian physician from New Orleans, who was engaged for yellow fever work, did a lot of wonderful surgical work in addition. Dr Parker, who had passed through several epidemics in New Orleans, caught the Cuban variety of yellow fever, but recovered.

No more in our shack came down with the yellow fever, though Mr Rathom, who had been under observation at the fever hospital for several days, was finally declared to be infected, and went off on the train. One day Mr Ewan came back, discharged. He had had malarial fever and was cured. The same afternoon we saw Major Romeyn, a retired army officer, who had turned war correspondent, ride in that ominous freight car. The train made frequent trips now. "The Yellow Fever Express" we called it, and we wondered how many hundreds of thousands would eventually ride over that route into the interior. It was stated one morning that thirty-five new cases had broken out; the morning after that, six hundred; the third morning, two thousand.

During those days of truce at the front, many of the soldiers secured brief leave to tramp into Siboney for the purpose of buying things at the commissary store which could not be had out at the front. During these days we heard many stories about how Spanish sharpshooters had been "potted" by our boys. One of the colored regiments captured a Spanish sharpshooter on the first of July. They saved him a choice morsel to be "eaten" after the day's fighting was over. This prisoner had been known to pick off wounded men, and consequently he had no further claim on life. Such a fiend, if taken alive, is none the less marked for death.

The Spaniard was bound to a tree, and eight of the good shots of the regiment stood off at fair range, took aim and fired at the word. Eight balls went through that Spaniard's heart and the hole in his breast, through which all passed, was no bigger around than a man's thumb. A darkey who, smoking a black cigar of good odor, listened to some of the sharpshooting tales, told one of his own:

"Yo' see, gemmen, on de mawning' ob de second I was in a powerful bad way fo' a smoke. I done got a chance to tote out after sharpshooters, and I done took it mighty quick. Yo' see, I done thought if I could pot a Spaniard, maybe he'd hab some seegyars on his pusson. Gorra-mighty, but I done had good luck, fo' I cotched two ob dem Spaniards, an' when I got em I done went through dair clothes. De fust didn't hab no seegyars. He was a Spanish pirate, fo' shuuah. But de second was a Spanish gen'leman—he had fo' seegyars—and dis one I'se smoking is de last ob de lot."

There was another story told of a soldier and his "bunkie". Our men on the march each carry half of a small tent, known officially as a shelter tent, but designated variously by the soldier as a "dog-tent" or a "pup-house". The tent is just large enough for two soldiers to crawl under and go to sleep. These two men are each other's "bunkies", and as is natural under the circumstances, they generally become fast friends. If you injure a soldier you injure his "bunkie" and instead of one man to fight you have two.

Now, this soldier and his "bunkie" were side by side at San Juan. The "bunkie" fell wounded; he was so badly hurt that it was out of the question for him alone to get back to the first dressing station. Therefore his tent-mate went with him, supporting him at every step of the way. They had gone a few hundred yards when a sharpshooter's ball struck the wounded soldier and killed him in an instant. The surviving soldier laid the dead one on the ground, pressed his hand tenderly, then knelt beside him. While in this exposed position two more bullets came that way, but without doing any harm. By the time the second had been fired, the living soldier had an idea where the sharpshooter pest was located. He began wriggling over the ground in that direction and soon had the sharp-shooter located to a certainty. He took a long and careful aim through his gun-sight. The Spanish soldier came toppling out of the tree, but that wasn't enough. The soldier stole through the grass and chapparal until he came to the base of the tree which had furnished a perch for the sharpshooter. Here he found the Spaniard, with a hole through the left breast, dead.

Probably the nerviest case of bringing down a sharpshooter was the performance of one of our teamsters. The men who drove the army wagons were not supposed to have arms, but after a few specimens of the enemy's tactics they provided themselves with revolvers.

This particular teamster was driving on a wagon when,

ahead of him, he heard the sharp crack of a rifle. In an instant he pulled up his mules to listen. Soon there was another crack.

Immediately the driver got down from his seat, drew his revolver from an inside pocket and prowled in the direction of the shots. After some time and a good deal of trouble the driver found his man. The Spaniard was perched up in a tree, all but hidden by the foliage. He was peering the other way.

"Thinks he's got someone ready to pot," muttered the prowler, and crept stealthily nearer. It would not do to chance a shot at too long a range with a revolver. But at last, still screened by bushes, and advancing with the quiet tread of a cat, the driver was near enough for a sure shot. He raised his revolver, just as the Spaniard raised his rifle to fire in some other direction. The revolver cracked first. Out of the tree tumbled the sharpshooter. Running forward with his revolver cocked, the driver made sure that his man was dead. Then he measured the distance from the foot of the tree to the spot from which he had fired. It was thirty-five yards!

On the second of July the bagging of the enemy's sharp-shooters was made more difficult and problematic from the fact that many of these pests dressed themselves in American uniforms stripped from the bodies of our dead soldiers. The only thing to admire about these brown marksmen was the brute courage they displayed in remaining hidden inside our lines and firing away, knowing that sooner or later their own death was inevitable.

One night the Spanish refugees from Santiago invaded

Siboney in search of rations. There was danger that they would bring in more yellow fever and they were soon hustled out of the town into a stretch of forest that ran from the pumping station out to Firmesa in the hills. Some of these people were frightfully emaciated, for when food ran low in Santiago the Spanish soldiers got most of it. Others had hideously distended stomachs, resulting from hunger and the consequent diet of water and green fruits. They were a pitiable lot. The sight of one skeleton baby of about eighteen months haunted me. There was nothing more than wizened skin over its little bones. Before I could find any suitable food for the child the refugees had been sent out of the town. The next morning I determined to do what was possible to relieve the worst cases among the refugees. It was necessary to have the support of someone with a more extended knowledge of Spanish than my own. Such a man was found in the Hon F B Genovar, state senator and mayor of St Augustine, Florida. He was an official member of the expedition, having come as interpreter to General Shafter. A gentleman who combined big-heartedness, wide experience, thorough knowledge of the Spanish race and fluency in their language, Senator Genovar was just the one for such an expedition. He consented in an instant. He had already done a world of good among our own sick. While the Senator provided himself with a big supply of quinine, I obtained a quantity of malted milk up at the Red Cross hospital.

A short walk brought us to the pumping station. Just on the other side of the shallow stream refugees were dipping up water into all sorts of containers. A few steps beyond and we were in the thick of their encampment. It lay along either side of a shaded road, in one of the most picturesque places imaginable. Some of the people had no shelter; others had slight lean-tos made of boughs; a few families had what were, under the circumstances, really ambitious huts. Those who were well enough to eat army rations had been supplied. Many were afflicted with malarial and other fevers, and the senator was soon busy doling out quinine, accompanying the doses with voluble directions. The skeleton baby I could not find now, but there were other cases fully as pitiful. One of them was a young woman who had arrived the day before from Santiago. On the way she had given birth to a child. Somehow she got as far as this camp. She lay under the shelter of a few boughs, her child swathed in the few rags she could find. The poor mother, unable to touch hearty food, had eaten nothing since the birth. Her companions showed the most selfish indifference. They did not even stir themselves to get hot water at our request. Nearby there was a guard squad of Michigan volunteers, posted there to keep the people from going in to Siboney. They were prompt and sympathetic. While one built a little fire, another found a tomato can, washed it, filled it with water and set it on the fire. In a few minutes it was boiling. In this we dissolved malted milk and gave the drink to the weakened, famished mother. She drank it greedily. Not deeming it wise to trust any of the milk powder with the woman's companions, we gave sufficient of it to the soldiers, who promised to see that it was prepared and given to the mother at regular intervals. Further on we found children and people equally in need of malted milk. The quinine went off with the speed of a war extra. For hours we went on through the camp. The misery there was appalling. There were many here who were wealthy and well supplied with money and jewelry, but they displayed little desire to be charitable to their less fortunate fellow-citizens. There were few well-dressed people in the throng, though there was plenty of tawdry finery. The print wrapper was the most popular form of dress among the women. On some of these wrappers were bedraggled but valuable laces. Though the American government furnished army rations in abundance, some of the wealthy ones had brought along baskets of silver plate to barter for food. Despite the popular notion of Spanish feminine beauty, few of these women were beautiful. In a blockhouse near Siboney, however, we found a girl of perhaps fifteen who possessed genuine beauty. She was attended by an old female domestic. We sought out the officer of the guard and urged him to see to it that no harm came to her. He replied by taking us into the guard-house and pointing to the upper story of the little building. On one of the lower slopes of the rude staircase that led up to the woman's room sat a sentinel. The officer added, simply, that the honor of the American army was pledged for the girl's safety. This formed a striking contrast to the stories which are told of the treatment of women who fall into the hands of Spanish soldiers.

While we were out we became thirsty, and we searched for

a drink of the most cooling beverage that is to be found in Cuba—the milk of the green cocoanut. There were plenty of Cubans about, and we made a trade with a Cuban *sargente.* These self-important non-commissioned offers always have a body-servant in the form of a boy of fifteen or sixteen. We paid twenty cents to the *sargente*; the boy did the work. Kicking off his canvas shoes, the boy ascended a cocoanut palm. In a twinkling green cocoanuts began to come down to the ground. Then the boy came down and with his machete opened the cocoanuts. The milk was delicious and cool. A party of our soldiers passing joined us in the drink. The natives use the ripe cocoanuts. They grind the pulp, mix it with a goodly proportion of sugar, and stew it for hours, until it is a thoroughly cooked paste. This they bake into cakes, which they call cocoanut bread. To a lover of sweets it is delicious. In marked contrast to the abundance of food in Siboney were the famished appetites of soldiers who came in from the front, where the long truce was dragging on, with only an hour's fighting on the tenth of July by way of variation. No soldier who came by the correspondents' mess table at meal time passed by hungry. The only condition imposed was that officers and enlisted men must sit democratically at the same table.

General Miles' arrival in Siboney was meteoric. He went through the town and out to the front before many were aware of his presence. Like a meteor, he left a trail of fire behind. It took the form of a peremptory order to burn Siboney—something that should have been done more than a fortnight before. A cloud of smoke, then a burst of flame, showed up at one corner of the town. From house to house went the soldiers, working enthusiastically under their officers. They made a picnic of this sanctioned incendiarism. Bad as the outbreak of yellow fever already was, these fiery tactics doubtless saved many Americans' lives. The Cubans denounced us as being "worse than Weyler". There was a grievance behind their "kick". Following in the wake of our soldiers, they had garnered in a rich harvest of clothing, blankets, *ponchos*, haversacks and other things which our soldiers had thrown aside on going into a fight and had never found again. This plunder was stored in the Siboney houses, for the most part carefully concealed. The devastating tongue of flame left the Cubans as poor as they had been before the arrival of the Yankee trooper.

Our own shack was one of the first buildings to go. We lived under canvas once more, as we had lived at Daiquiri.

Mr Ewan and myself made our home in a seven by seven tent, in which were two canvas cots and considerable baggage. During our very first night under canvas we were treated to a sample of the wickedness of which a Cuban storm is capable. Preceded by crashes of thunder, which made the roar of the *Oregon*'s thirteen-inch guns seem tame, the rain came down as if the bottom had dropped out of the sky. The incessant flashes of lightning took on a bright purple hue. The water soon came through the canvas. Cots and blankets soon became soaked. A sagging at the sides of our tent showed that some of the guy-rope pins had been washed out of the ground, and our tiny home was threatened with collapse. The torrents were yet too heavy for us to go outside and drive in the wooden pins. One of us sat at the back of the tent, and one at the front, each holding up a pole in the frantic effort to keep the tent upright. When that fearful storm abated somewhat, we drew on our *ponchos*, ran outside and hastily drove the guy-rope pins in again. All around us were tents blown flat by the gale. Then we got inside and lay in soaked clothes, on soaked bedding, until morning. There were few correspondents in Siboney at this time. There were a few out at the front, a greater number were sick, and the remainder had already gone back to the United States on returning transports. When we awoke in the morning it was still raining. The mess servants were nowhere to be seen. There was no sign of breakfast, no chance to build a fire on which to cook one. I ran to our kitchen tent, got a few hard-tack crackers and, wet and disconsolate, we chewed at these until a voice outside our tent observed: "I'm —, of Washington. Just got down on the *Catania*. I haven't any tent but I've got two bottles of—"

Before he could say any more two pairs of arms reached out and pulled him inside. A second correspondent from Washington materialized, and we four passed the morning in a condition of jolly misery. There were plenty of good things on the *Catania*, including matches, of which the commissary had run out. It was once more possible to smoke as often as we wished.

On the fourteenth of July the city of Santiago surrendered, though it was not until three days later that our flag was hoisted over the municipal buildings. On the 14th, therefore, journalistic interest in Santiago practically ceased. On that day the *Seneca* left Siboney to return to the United States. I was one of ten or twelve correspondents who were glad of the chance to get back to the United States and rest for the Havana campaign, which we then supposed was to follow. Senator Genovar was one of our party. As we sailed out of Siboney bay we gave three cheers for home. Then our hearts saddened at the thought of the thousands of fine specimens of America's best manhood left behind there, a prey to disease. Before we sailed Senator Genovar found on the beach several sacks of mail addressed to different points in the United States. He notified the ship's officers, who had heard nothing of them, and they were sent for and taken aboard. The postal arrangements with the Fifth Army Corps was as poor, as crude and as lacking in system as could possibly be imagined. This was not true at first, while Postmaster Eben Brewer remained alive and well. He was a zealous, competent official, and things went smoothly under him, but as much cannot be said of his assistant, who took charge of things when the jovial, helpful Brewer fell ill of yellow fever, of which he afterward died.

The thought of the voyage home on the *Seneca* will always be a melancholy one to me. In army vernacular, the *Seneca* is known as "the first of the horror ships." The story of that fearful trip must ever be a distinct and accusing chapter in the depths of official incompetence of which the politics-infested American government is capable. Fifty or sixty wounded and disease-shattered men came back with us. There were next to no medicines; despite the fact that the commissary at Siboney was well stocked, there was so little food on the *Seneca* that the passengers were compelled to subsist on two scanty meals per day. The water aboard was two months old. In a glass of it a thick red precipitate would settle. Wounded men often asked wistfully for a glass of "white water". And this was in the tropics, with a ship's load of feverish men!

There were two young and inexperienced contract doctors aboard. Thought it was confidently expected that yellow fever would break out among us on the way north, neither had a thermometer for taking patients' temperatures. It has been claimed by the surgical department of the army that only men able to walk were taken aboard the ship. I know from my own observation how utterly false that statement was. There were many men who could not sit up; men who fainted when it became necessary for them to make an effort to transfer to the health boat alongside in lower New York bay. Men had their wounds bathed in salt water, because there was no fresh water. Wounds were necessarily so neglected that amazing quantities of pus were taken out of them when they reached New York. There was a heroine aboard in Miss Jeanette Jennings, a Red Cross nurse, who took devoted care of the men and nourished them as far as possible with a few delicacies gotten hastily from the Red Cross ship when she realized what utter lack there was of every provision on the *Seneca*. There was a hero aboard, Captain Dowdy, USA, who was Miss Jennings' right-hand support in everything. There were others, who helped all they could. And there were foreign attachés on board, who saw and observed as was their mission. It would cause Americans acute shame could they read the reports which these attachés turned in to their respective governments. It is not necessary to go further into details of that tragic voyage home. The people cannot yet have forgotten the *Seneca*. I saw no exaggeration in any printed statements. It does not seem that there could be any exaggeration of the infamous way in which our sick and wounded soldiers were brought home.

The public, too, will remember the tales of incompetence and lack of provision amounting to positive cruelty—which were told of the treatment of our victorious army at Camp Wikoff. I went down to Camp Wikoff to see if things were as bad as they were pictured in the press. They were worse. One night I sat there in the doorway of the tent, looking down the slope upon a regiment of what were once as fine physical men as ever went out of the United States. They were shattered beyond recognition. In the group around the doorway of that tent were young officers not long out of West Point. There were also officers who had been in the army in the days of '61. All knew alike what should have been; all knew what had been.

## The End

# Also available from The Clapton Press:

**BOADILLA by Esmond Romilly**
The nephew that Winston Churchill disowned describes his experiences fighting with the International Brigade in the Battle of Madrid. Written on his honeymoon in St. Jean de Luz after eloping with Jessica Mitford.

**MY HOUSE IN MALAGA by Sir Peter Chalmers Mitchell**
While most ex-pats fled to Gibraltar in 1936, Sir Peter stayed on to protect his house and servants from the fascists. He ended up in prison for sheltering Arthur Koestler from Franco's rabid head of propaganda, who had threatened to "shoot him like a dog".

**SOME STILL LIVE by F.G. Tinker Jr.**
Frank G. Tinker was a US pilot who signed up with the Republican forces because he didn't like Mussolini. He was also attracted by the prospect of adventure and a generous pay cheque. This is an account of his experiences in Spain.

**SPANISH PORTRAIT by Elizabeth Lake**
A brutally honest, semi-autobiographical novel set in San Sebastian and Madrid between 1934 and 1936, portraying a frantic love affair against a background of apprehension and confusion as Spain drifted inexorably towards civil war.

**MARGUERITE REILLY by Elizabeth Lake**
First published in 1946, Marguerite Reilly is the fictionalised story of four generations of Irish immigrants struggling to make good in the Victorian and post-Victorian era, from the days of the Great Hunger up to the end of the second world war. Harrowing at times but always entertaining, this is a must-read for anyone with Anglo-Irish heritage.

**BEHIND THE SPANISH BARRICADES**
**by John Langdon-Davies, with a Prologue by Paul Preston**
First published in 1936, *Behind the Spanish Barricades* chronicles the early months of the Spanish Civil War through the eyes of a seasoned journalist well acquainted with Spanish and Catalan cultures. Arriving on a second-hand motorbike, he experiences the exuberant atmosphere in Barcelona during its short-lived proletarian revolution, as well as the horrors of war as he visits Toledo during the siege of the Alcázar.

# Also available from The Clapton Press:

**NEVER MORE ALIVE: INSIDE THE SPANISH REPUBLIC**
**by Kate Mangan, with a Preface by Paul Preston**
When her lover, the German refugee Jan Kurzke, made his way to Spain to join the International Brigade in October 1936, Kate Mangan went after him. She ended up working with Constancia de la Mora in the Republic's Press Office, where she met a host of characters including WH Auden, Stephen Spender, Ernest Hemingway, Robert Capa, Gerda Taro, Walter Reuter and many more. When Jan was seriously injured she visited him in hospital, helped him across the border to France and left him with friends in Paris so she could return to her job in Valencia.
"Ever since I first read the manuscript about fifteen years ago, I have longed to see this wonderful book in print" - Paul Preston

**THE GOOD COMRADE, MEMOIRS OF AN INTERNATIONAL BRIGADER**
**by Jan Kurzke, with an Introduction by Richard Baxell**
Jan Kurzke was a left-wing artist who fled Nazi Germany in the early 1930s and tramped round the south of Spain, witnessing first-hand the poverty of the rural population, later moving to England where he met Kate Mangan. When the Spanish civil war broke out in 1936, Jan went back and joined the International Brigade, while Kate followed shortly after, working for the Republican press office. Many of his fellow volunteers died in the savage battles on the outskirts of Madrid and Jan himself was seriously wounded at Boadilla, nearly losing his leg. This is his memoir, a companion volume to *Never More Alive*.

**IN PLACE OF SPLENDOUR: THE AUTOBIOGRAPHY OF A SPANISH WOMAN by Constancia de la Mora,**
**with a foreword by Soledad Fox Maura**
Constancia de la Mora was the grand-daughter of Antonio Maura, who had served under Alfonso XIII as Prime Minister. She was one of the first women to obtain a divorce under the fledgling Spanish Republic. During the civil war she became a key figure in the Republic's International Press Office, moving to the USA and Mexico after the war was lost. This is her remarkable memoir, with a detailed history of the build-up to the conflict.

# Also available from The Clapton Press:

**FIRING A SHOT FOR FREEDOM: THE MEMOIRS OF FRIDA STEWART**
**with a foreword and afterword by Angela Jackson**
Frida Stewart was a graduate of the Royal College of Music who became involved with Aid for Spain during the Civil War and ended up driving an ambulance out to Murcia. She went on to Madrid where she worked for the Republican Press Office, visiting the front and "firing a shot for freedom". She was later in France when the Nazis invaded and was imprisoned in an internment camp, from which she escaped with a friend. This is her story, described by Paul Preston as "an utterly riveting and deeply moving memoir . . ."

**BRITISH WOMEN AND THE SPANISH CIVIL WAR**
**by Angela Jackson**
Through oral and written narratives, this book examines the interaction between women and the war in Spain, their motivation, the distinctive form of their involvement and the effect of the war on their individual lives. These themes are related to wider issues, such as the nature of memory and the role of women within the public sphere. The extent to which women engaged with this cause surpasses by far other instances of female mobilization in peace-time Britain. Such a phenomenon therefore can offer lessons to those who would wish to encourage a greater degree of interest amongst women in political activities today.

**www.theclaptonpress.com**